# THE BALLAD IN MUSIC

BY

SYDNEY NORTHCOTE
D.Mus. (Oxon.), Hon. A.R.C.M.

WITH A NOTE BY
MAURICE BROWN

OXFORD UNIVERSITY PRESS
LONDON NEW YORK TORONTO

OXFORD UNIVERSITY PRESS
AMEN HOUSE, E.C. 4
London Edinburgh Glasgow New York
Toronto Melbourne Capetown Bombay
Calcutta Madras
HUMPHREY MILFORD
PUBLISHER TO THE UNIVERSITY

First published 1942
Reprinted 1944

PRINTED IN GREAT BRITAIN

## TO MAURICE BROWN, ESQ.

*Dear Maurice,*

   *When you invited me to give a series of broadcast talks on the Ballad you did not foresee that I would 'father' a book on you. Neither did I. But the subject proved too alluring. Whether this essay was worth the trouble of its preparation remains to be seen. For you, at all events, it may be a happy reminder of the many discussions we had on the subject.*

S. N.

ADDISCOMBE, 1941

# CONTENTS

I. INTRODUCTION . . . . 1

II. EARLY BALLADS . . . . 14

III. MODERN BALLADS . . . . 44

IV. DIVERS BALLADS . . . . 79

V. CONCLUSIONS . . . . 94

BIBLIOGRAPHY . . . . 110

GRAMOPHONE RECORDS AND INDEX
with a note by MAURICE BROWN . . . 114

CHAPTER I

# INTRODUCTION

THE definition of the ballad, in music and literature alike, is indeed difficult, but not impossible. Professor Ker's remarks are worth quoting: 'In spite of Socrates and his logic we may venture to answer the question "What is ballad?" by saying—"Ballad is the *Milldams of Binnorie* and *Sir Patrick Spens* and *The Douglas Tragedy* and *Lord Randal* and *Childe Maurice* and things of that sort" '; a delightful evasion which is more like a description than a definition. Unfortunately, the lexicographical association of the word (Lat. *ballare*, to dance) affords little help. Instead it serves only to confound. Even if it were possible to trace its origin back to some form of communal folk-dance, as some theorists have tried to do, it would only add to the confusion already gathered about the term. For its extended use, both in music and in literature, already furnishes enough diversity.

However, a brief review of the literary usage may provide some basis for defining the qualifications of the ballad in music, beyond which any exceptions to the rule may be dealt with as they arise. Sir Walter Scott, in his *Minstrelsy of the Scottish Border* (1802–3) and elsewhere, seems to affirm that the foundation of the study of ballads was laid in Britain, and their influence on our modern romantic poetry can hardly be exaggerated. In Germany, through Scott's work and Percy's *Reliques*, the ballad has exercised just as powerful an influence on the national literature, and in music its significance in the progress of the German *Lied* was considerable.

1

In the meantime the usage of another form of the word, 'ballade', must be noticed, although it does not concern the present study. It is applied to an entirely distinct form of verse. Henri de Croi, in his *L'Art et science de rhetorique* (1493), has laid down the rules for this form of ballade. It consists of three stanzas and an envoi, with a refrain repeated after each stanza and after the envoi. Its origin may be traced to the *Canzone di ballo* of the Italians, although its modern form originates in Provençal literature. It flourished prolifically in France from the reign of Charles V until the end of the sixteenth century, and boasts such illustrious names as Machault, Froissart, Deschamps, de Pison, Chartier, Baude, François Villon, Marot, Voiture, Sarrazin, and la Fontaine. After falling out of fashion for two centuries it again became popular through Theodore de Banville, who published his *Trente-six ballades joyeuses* in 1873. A typical French form of poetry, it found little or no favour elsewhere except in Britain. The distinguishing characteristic of the medieval English ballades and those of Chaucer is the omission of the envoi. Gower's ballades are written in French. From the sixteenth century it fell into disfavour, as in France. Then came the work of Swinburne, Lang, Dobson, Gosse, and W. E. Henley in this form. In our own day we have the several successful examples of G. K. Chesterton. Musically, this form of ballade is a notable feature of French song.

The narrative ballad[1] with which this essay is principally concerned can furnish no such definite rules or so strict a form. It can boast, however, an uninterrupted existence

[1] To avoid confusion with the French ballade, the spelling 'ballad' without the final *e* is used throughout the book to refer to the narrative form.

down to the present day. Undoubtedly, the origins of this particular phase of literature must also be sought in the distant past. But in the search for these disputed origins the natural conditions and processes of poetic creation need not be distorted. Yet, as Earle Welby[1] has observed, 'the ballad has inspired more learned and ingenious nonsense than anything in English poetry'. The notion that ballads were transmitted orally even after the advent of printing is something more than mere theory. It is an undeniable fact. That under such conditions they naturally suffered or enjoyed modifications of all kinds is fairly obvious. Any critical consideration of such variants is not called for here, and in any case, to judge by the many opinions of scholars, it would only be a matter of considerable controversy.

Much of the critical discussion seems to have centred around the supposed authorship of the ballads. Are they 'aristocratic' or 'popular' in origin? Are they the work of unknown poets or minstrels, or is every ballad a communal or concerted effort? Common sense must be the guiding factor. No ballad has an original text until comparatively modern times. It was something which was listened to, not written or read. That is a very important point. As to the quality or quantity of the original authorship, it is better that criticism should be practical rather than ingenious. There seems nothing unusual in the idea of a minstrel improvising a story to earn his supper or a bed, and then leaving it to the tender mercies and uncertain memories of his hearers to pass it on with casual variants and, perhaps, a touch of local colour. I am quite prepared to find that some ballads had their source in the nobleman's hall and others in the market-

[1] T. Earle Welby, *English Poetry* (Methuen).

place or the country fair. The characteristics of both are similar enough. To quote Earle Welby again, 'Ballad does not differ from ballad as a poem by Shelley differs from one by Keats, or one by Tennyson from one by Swinburne'.[1] And the fact that certain variants of the same ballad are peculiar to certain counties or districts proves nothing beyond the fact that a story may lose or gain much in its travels. The variants themselves are all expressions of the same fundamental, a ballad. They differ in detail, but not in style or form. They may differ in characteristics, but not in kind.

How, then, are we to define ballad? What is certain is that it is a story told in the simplest poetic manner. It is a popular form of poetry. Its impersonal character is more or less implicit in the fact that it is pure narrative, and its simplicity both in metre and in construction is a necessary requirement for its oral transmission, and, furthermore, is just that particular quality which gives it the directness of expression which is often one of its highest achievements.

Thus far the data for a definition seems clear enough. The term 'ballad' may be applied to any type of narrative verse, generally written in simple stanzas; verse which is descriptive rather than reflective, and expressive rather than introspective. Its character is essentially impersonal and, in the simplest sense of the word, dramatic. Moreover, its very nature (without any regard for particular theories of authorship) indicates that it was a popular form of poetic entertainment, and, as such, would easily take to itself all those simple evidences of popular appeal, such as refrains or the apparently unnecessary repetition of lines, and, of course, the inevitable variants of an

[1] Op. cit.

unwritten text. Its form depends therefore on a natural continuity of situation and event rather than the logic of reflection or sentiment, a fact which suggests an influence on the musical form. Within the limits of such a definition, it will be said, almost anything may happen. The answer is obvious. It did.

Although the ancient ballad may not fulfil the definitiveness of a circumscribed poetic form, it does furnish a few peculiarities which are very interesting. The numbers three, seven, and nine seem to have a quaint frequency and significance.

He's taken three locks of her yellow hair.

*Binnorie.*

When in and came her seven brothers.

*Clerk Saunders.*

And in a den spied nine dead men.

*The Dowie Houms of Yarrow.*

Common objects are invariably described as being made of silver or of gold.

Hung fifty siller bells and nine.

*Thomas the Rhymer.*

The mast was of the beaten gold. . . .
The anchor of the silver sheen.

*Lass of Lochroyan.*

The story nearly always starts abruptly. There is no preamble. The action begins at once and its continuity is maintained by the simplest expedients. The use of familiar phrases to indicate time and distance is another common feature.

Up then crew the red, red cock.

*Wife of Usher's Well.*

Three months and a day were gone.

*Fair Annie.*

5

They hadna' sailed a league, a league,
A league but barely three.

*Sir Patrick Spens.*

The absence of a sense of humour, except of the grim kind, is also noticeable. The humorous ballad was a very much later product. Religion, strangely enough, is rarely mentioned, except in the vaguest manner.

It would seem, then, that the definition of the ballad so far is logical enough, and at the same time wide enough to allow sufficient scope for poetic treatment without any undue limitations in form or structure. The narrative may be heroic, mythological, legendary, national, historical, satirical, romantic, or pure fantasy. Moreover, if further distinctions are desired, there are the convenient categories of dramatic, historical, and pastoral ballads, and so on. And, to be perfectly logical, there seems no reason for the exclusion of personal narrative.

Unfortunately, poets have frequently used the term ballad for poems which cannot possibly be considered as narrative. Even if it is supposed that in such cases the word-derivation led to its use for 'a song accompanied by or accompanying a dance', the situation may be reduced to complete absurdity by calling the modern fox-trot lyric a ballad. And surely *Hark, hark the Lark* is not a ballad because Schubert set it to a German dance measure! Again, it is difficult to see why Percy in his *Reliques* should describe *Sumer is icumen in* as the 'earliest ballad now remaining in the English language'. To me it seems anything but a ballad. I was not aware that the music had anything to do with dancing, and if it had I should be inclined to regret the waste of such excellent counterpoint.

It may be argued that the word could carry a secondary

meaning. But 'a song accompanied by or accompanying a dance' is too much like a generalization. It lacks the significance of a definition. In any case, it would seem more logical to follow Morley's example[1] in such cases, and use the term 'Ballets'[2] wherever the characteristic of narrative is entirely absent.

The literary snobbishness which uses 'Ballad-poetry' as a patronizing title for anonymous popular poetry of all kinds is to be deplored. However humble the possible origin of the ballad, it is too vital to despise. Admittedly, the intrinsic value of any ballad as poetry is not necessarily high. Which is not to say it may not have begun as a simple poem of real artistic merit. But 'all that the people had to do with the ballad was to vulgarize it, to bring each example nearer to an average, depriving the poem of some of the marks of its individual authorship'.[3] Often enough, a phrase here and there will betray all the lineaments of great poetry, suggesting the authentic among the corrupt. To suppose that this implies the reverse is not so feasible, since it would run counter to the natural existence of the ballad as popular entertainment. And editing which could so ably reconstruct some lines would hardly permit some of the grosser crudities which remain. On the other hand, the splendid ballad of *Edward* has come to us so free from primitive phrasing and coarseness as to suggest either a very surprisingly unaltered original or some 'distinguished restoration'.

In any event, the influence of such a *corpus* of vital

---

[1] *Vide* Morley's *Plaine and easie introduction to Practical Musicke* (1597): 'there is another kind . . . which they tearm *Ballete* or daunces, and are songs which being sung to a dittie may likewise be danced . . .'.
[2] In Coverdale's Bible (1535) the Song of Solomon was entitled 'Salomon's Balettes, called Cantica Canticorum'.
[3] Earle Welby, op. cit.

poetry—its vitality is implicit in its avowed popularity—cannot be denied. Its virtues are self-evident, and its faults the very natural outcome of its precarious existence. Lacking the preparation and certainty of a written text, it was sturdy enough to survive all the consequent ravages of the unwritten. At its best, it has a striking fundamental strength, if only in the simple directness of its expression and the vivid swiftness of its action. Examples like *Clerk Saunders* and *Edward*, to name only two, have all the power and merit of great poetry. And there will be few who would deny the same virtue, in some degree, to such examples as *Fair Annie*, *The Wife of Usher's Well*, *Sir Patrick Spens*, *The Queen's Marie*, *The Lass of Lochroyan*, *Edom O'Gordon*, *Thomas the Rhymer*, and *Binnorie*. If the poetic content of the modern examples by Scott, Thomson, Campbell, Swinburne, Davidson, Coleridge, Rossetti, Morris, and others is of a higher order, it is also true that the dramatic power of the older examples is not so far behind. Whether some of the moderns will enjoy the longevity of the ancients remains to be proved. The old ballads were created for performance, the new for reading. And the latter have the additional disadvantage of existing in a somewhat unappreciative age.

But what of the troubadour, the minstrel, the ballad-monger, call him what you will? To him, and perhaps to him alone, the early ballad owes its very existence. In many cases he would be the original poet, as

> High placed in hall, a welcome guest,
> He poured to lord and lady gay
> The unpremeditated lay.

A creature of circumstance, he was petted in one age and persecuted in another. He has come down to us as a romantic and, at times, an unreal figure. He has no counterpart in our own day.[1] Yet it is not difficult to imagine an age when such wandering minstrels were welcome callers at the nobleman's castle, to entertain the gentle guests with the latest song and story, and, perhaps, the local gossip, too. Or at a country fair, carrying the news they had gathered on their travels, to relate it in 'measured song' to a crowd as yet unspoiled by the sensations of a daily press or the blandishments of the twopenny fiction library. The Welsh Bard, the Danish Scald, the German Meistersinger and Minnesinger, the French Troubadour, Trouvère, and Jongleur, are all of the same honourable tribe. Among them would be found poets, musicians, actors, and dancers, and sometimes a combination of all four. The legend of Blondin, on the one hand, and the edict of Elizabeth (in which 'minstrels, wandering abroad', were classed with 'rogues, vagabonds, and sturdy beggars'), on the other, are indicative of their shifting fortunes. Percy's essay on the ancient minstrel in his *Reliques* is an entertaining account to which the reader may be referred. It is obvious that the minstrel, whether of high or low degree, had always to face the sternest of all tests, constant performance. Whether the tale was his own, or the remembered effort of another, it had to win popular approval. No doubt there were certain very popular ballads in constant demand. They would be in the repertoire of all. And then

> Each blank, in faithless memory void,
> The poet's glowing thought supplied.

The ballad-monger, as such, was probably a lowly order of minstrel, belonging entirely to the common people and visiting the village inn and the fair. He was, in point of environment and age, an aftermath of the

[1] Except in the East.

travelling minstrel. He would probably combine with his minstrelsy some form of itinerant trading, a travelling-jack, a tinker, or some other ready means of a livelihood. Or he might even profess to tell fortunes or cure 'divers ills'. There must be many like myself who treasure dim childish memories of such a quaint character. Looking back a century or two, it would be easy to visualize him as a familiar creature of the age. He would be a carrier of news, eagerly listened to: and he would shrewdly measure the significance of some local gossip to supply him with a new story at his next port of call. His poetry and music would be of the crudest sort. He needed nothing more than a ready facility in doggerel verse, and the ability to adapt it to the rhythms of some familiar tunes, generally dance tunes. Here, then, we have the ballad in its rudi-mentary state, virtually uncultured, but combining the dual character of narrative and dance as if by accident. An example like *Widdecombe Fair* is probably typical of this sort of thing. Admittedly, much of this is pure con-jecture, and it may be objected that it raises the activities of an itinerant musician at a country fair to the level of the true minstrel. But is it not equally reasonable to see in this 'ragged remnant of ancient minstrelsy' the last echoes of the established customs of former days? It is a characteristic which is by no means confined to our own country. There is ample evidence that popular dance-tunes served for the singing of narrative poems in many countries. It is easy to realize that the lilt of a well-known tune would be a real aid in the improvisation of a 'rhymed story'. And it may be discovered that the widely differing verbal texts to many of our own folk-songs have a somewhat unexpected significance.

At this point it will be convenient to refer to the loose

use of the word 'ballad' as a title for all kinds of folk-songs. It adds yet another difficulty to the confusion already noted. Very often, these folk-songs would seem to have no connexion either with the narrative ideal or with the dance. But they cannot be ruled out of the present discussion, although their consideration adds but little to the conclusions which I hope to reach ultimately. For that typically English product, the Ballad Opera, cannot be ignored. Like its German counterpart, the *Singspiel*, it is national enough and distinctive enough to have a significant title. At first view, if we accept the preliminary definition of the ballad already suggested, the title of ballad would seem to be a complete misnomer, unless the extension in the meaning of the word is to leave it with no meaning at all. But a closer examination of the musical and poetical evolution of the word may lead to a different conclusion. Therefore, when the ballad opera and folk-songs *alias* ballads have their place in a subsequent discussion, it will be to advance a theory for the justness of the title, without detriment to a definition which endeavours to give to the ballad the significance it deserves.

When the composer takes the place of the minstrel a different set of conditions must inevitably arise. But again there is a difficulty. Examples from the eighteenth century cannot be linked with those of the following century because of the very different ideals behind them. Broadly, the earlier composers were not concerned with any search for an art form, but were content to maintain the older tradition, with such modifications as were the natural consequence of their times. It was only when the German, Carl Loewe, began his composition of ballads that its consideration as an art form was at all possible.

For the sake of clarity, therefore, I have given the title of 'Modern Ballads' to my consideration of the ballad as an art form, and the earlier compositions must take their relative position among the early ballads. They follow the ballad opera, of course. The ideal of narrative is never absent in the modern ballad, and from Loewe to Wolf it maintains a certain distinction in form and style which is well worth close study. Moreover, other countries have their own characteristic contributions to this phase of song to make for interesting comparison.

It is important to observe a striking parallel in the revival of poetic and musical interest in the ballad and the ballade. The poetic awakening, not unnaturally, comes first, and belongs to the close of the eighteenth century. Its musical counterpart came soon after the turn of the century. This is not the place to anticipate arguments which will arise later in the course of this essay. But it is a sad fact that there were no English composers ready to take up the renaissance of song which was witnessed in Germany and in France, as well as in Russia. English song had to wait until the days of Parry and Stanford before it won its present significance. The modern ballade,[1] which is mainly though not entirely confined to French song, lies outside the scope of the present discussion, of course, but modern examples of the narrative ballad are both numerous and varied.

Unfortunately composers, like poets, were inclined to be indiscriminate in their use of the title of ballad. Choral ballads are obvious enough and suggest a convenient and effective presentation of a lengthy narrative. But the use of the term for instrumental compositions, from piano solos to orchestral movements, is not so easy to define or to

---

[1] In its French spelling, not as the German word.

defend. And when to this is added the prevalence of the drawing-room ballad the confusion is complete. Subsequently, it will be seen that I have grouped these several usages of the word under the title of 'Divers Ballads'. There was no other way.

The scheme of this essay is now apparent. There will be those who, finding no fault with the logic of its presentation, will criticize the inclusion of widely different activities under a single heading. For example, it may be argued that the choral ballad takes a more fitting place with the modern ballad. I hesitated myself on this point. My only reason for separating them was that song forms have certain definite characteristics which are in contrast to those of choral forms.

In any event, it will not affect the main argument of the book. This may be stated simply as a plea for the study of the ballad in music as an art form, after dismissing (although first considering) other manifestations of various kinds. As an art form, the ballad in music is seen at its truest and best in the modern ballad and the choral ballad. To put my aim in another form, the object of this essay is to put forward the same argument for the ballad in music as was expressed by Earle Welby[1] for the ballad in poetry when he said 'it is extremely desirable that the ballad should be studied, not as a really or reputedly very ancient curiosity,[2] but as a vital and permanently interesting form of poetry'.

[1] Op. cit.
[2] In some of the Balkan countries, the recitation of poetic narratives to the accompaniment of some native instrument claims a tradition which goes back to the days of Homer.

## CHAPTER II

# EARLY BALLADS

IT has been asserted by some scholars that the ancient ballads had a communal authorship, being composed, as it were, at a public meeting! Others express the opinion that they were the work of an 'improviser, assisted by the crowd'. Both opinions seem so contrary to the normal process of poetic creation that one wonders why they were ever put forward at all. Presumably, the evidence for the suggestions is largely textual, and comes from a close analysis of the manuscripts of those old narrative poems which have been discovered. But it is questionable whether these transcribed ballads can ever have the authority of 'originals'. Transcription was the last thing the minstrel would desire. The individuality of his improvisation was undoubtedly his strongest appeal. It is significant that the advent of printing was the beginning of his downfall, and when 'broadsheet' ballads were sold at a penny each the days of minstrelsy were ended. Very probably, then, these transcribed texts are far removed from the original poems, having suffered all the modifications and mutilations which any poem would suffer after generations of oral transmission. As they stand, it is probably true enough that they were the work of a crowd—*of minstrels.*

Although the minstrel had fallen into such grave disrepute by the end of the sixteenth century, there is no doubt that for some centuries his rather chequered career had given him, at times, a position of real distinction and no little power. The Church always frowned upon him, in greater or lesser degree. And the opposition of the State was bound to follow when his influence with the crowd became politically inconvenient. It is generally believed that the Peasants' Rising of 1381, that of Jack Cade some seventy years later, as well as many other local riots, owed much to the influence of the minstrel. In any case, the history of minstrelsy cannot be summarized in a paragraph. It can go back as far as the Anglo-Saxon poem *Widsuth*. For the moment, it is no mere assumption that the minstrel came of a race of poets, actors, and musicians of real ability and learning. Some were probably attached as distinguished servants to royal and noble households with all the cultural benefits implicit in such patronage. (The word itself is derived from the Latin *minister*, a servant.) There would be those who were welcome guests at castle and hall, as well as lower orders who entertained the more popular audiences at weddings and fairs and the like. The several guilds of minstrels, such as the *Pui* of Arras (1105), the Chester minstrels (*circa* 1210), the Guild of Paris (1321), John O'Gaunt's *Roy des Ministralx* (1380), and the London Guild (founded 1469 and destined to become after many changes the present Worshipful Company of Musicians), to name only a few, are indicative of their status and organization.

The age of minstrelsy stretches over a long period. It was an activity which must be regarded on its own terms, and against its own historical background. There are very good reasons for assuming that the ancient ballad is a product of minstrelsy. The improvisation of a narrative poem was, perhaps, the *raison d'être* of the early minstrel, and it was the common delight of his age. The interchange of ballads is surely not difficult to believe. Memory was eager enough in days of oral transmission, and where memory failed a quick wit would immediately fill the gap. Thus the varying texts which have survived, the widely differing versions of the same story, even the confusion of two different events (e.g. *Chevy Chase* and *The Battle of Otterburn*), are the natural results of contemporary conditions. When the musical implications come to be considered later, it will be to approach the question of authorship from a different angle. But in both cases it seems difficult to resist the claim of the minstrels themselves.

When the editor of the *Oxford Book of English Verse* is compelled to explain in his preface

'for convenience, . . . as well as to avoid a dispute-royal, I have gathered most of the ballads into the middle of the seventeenth century'

it will be seen how sceptical the scholars are with regard to the antiquity of the early ballad. To gather the primitive drama of the early ballad into a century already familiar with the complete dramatic genius of Shakespeare and his contemporaries may seem to some of us a little odd. Even as we read these old narratives we must feel, instinctively, that they belong to a remoter era. They precede Shakespeare rather than follow him. It is noteworthy that many of the 'ballads' cited by Shakespeare (e.g. *Willow, willow*; *Heartsease*; *Greensleeves*, &c.) are nearly always popular songs. From early Tudor times the title signified a song of the people, a folk-song. On the other hand, the literary remains from the Middle Ages to Chaucer would seem to indicate that story-telling was the fashion of those days. Chaucer's *Canterbury Tales* do not represent an ingenious formula for the presentation of a poem. They reflect the spirit of their age and, for our present purpose, carry the essential suggestion that

16

story-telling was a contemporary delight and, apparently, a fairly normal art. It will be remembered that Chaucer makes the Parson apologize for relating his tale in prose in these significant lines:

> . . . I am a Southren man
> I can nat geste—rum, ram, ruf—by lettre
> Ne, god wot, rym hold I but litel bettre
> And therefor, if yow list, I wol nat glose
> I wol yow telle a mery tale in prose.

Bishop Percy reminds us that nearly all the minstrels were 'characterised, by way of eminence, to have been "of the North Country"'. The inference is, I think, obvious. The 'rhymed story' was common enough as early as the fourteenth century at least. All this would seem to be strong evidence for the antiquity of the ballad. It has the virtue of being more reliable, perhaps, than the testimony of the available texts of these poems. There is no actual evidence that the historical ballads were improvised soon after the event which inspired them, but it is not a very unreasonable supposition. The original date would soon be distorted by the addition of up-to-date similes and allusions from generation to generation. The ultimate text, full of these additions and corruptions, can offer no indication of the original date of the ballad in question. Undoubtedly, in spirit and style the ballad is ancient enough.

However, the questions of authorship and antiquity may be left to the scholars to discuss. Despite all verbal anachronisms, these early ballads would seem to belong to a remoter age than the seventeenth century. The terse vividness of their action seems arid compared with the spacious, glowing tension of Elizabethan drama. Rather do they typify those latter medieval days of strange contradictions—an age when quaint chivalry and stark cruelty could exist side by side—an age to which minstrelsy rather than poetry (in the strict sense of the word) properly belonged.

These arguments may seem somewhat irrelevant in an essay on the ballad in music. But they have an important bearing on the question of one's attitude towards the subject, and, ultimately, a certain influence on the later art forms. Moreover, they are not to be ignored in tracing the evolution of the early ballad down to that unique product, the ballad opera. To regard these early ballads simply as poems is obviously mistaken. For the most important point about them is that they were improvisations. They were meant for performance rather than perusal. They relied on an immediate appeal to the imagination. They were presented with all the minstrel's ability in mime and gesture. *And they were sung.* The musical considerations will inevitably lead us into the domain of folk-song and there we may discover some important implications.

As dramatic improvisations the ancient ballads are striking and distinctive enough. Although there was no call to be brief, the minstrel wasted no time in digressions of any sort, and his moralizing is only incidental even when he permits himself to moralize at all. Very probably the original ballads were much longer than the transcriptions which have come down to us. Even so we are conscious of a real dramatic economy in the 'settings of a scene', a vivid terseness in description, all of which could be enhanced so easily in a good performance. The delineation of the dramatic characters rarely depended on detail. Again we have to remember that so much would be suggested in the actual performance. The narrative of

*Edward*, apart from being such excellently contrived dialogue, succeeds in establishing the two characters with astonishing clearness. Now and then we encounter an unexpected turn in this direction, as, for example, in the *Lass of Lochroyan* when the 'rank reiver' says:

> Now are ye Queen of Heaven hie
>     Come to pardon a' our sin?
> Or are ye Mary Magdalen,
>     Was born at Bethlehem?

The subtle variations in the tempo of the narrative of *Clerk Saunders* are worth noting. For example, after the first of the seven brothers, who came in 'wi' torches burning red', had declared that his was the sword which should slay the sleeping Saunders, the ultimate killing is delayed while five of the brothers hesitate and express, in successive stanzas, their varying sentiments. It is this delay which gives to the following verse such a powerful sense of climax.

> Then up and gat the seventh of them
>     And never a word spake he;
> But he had striped his bright brown brand
>     Out through Clerk Saunders' fair bodye.

And the pathos of the scene where Margaret follows the ghost of her lover to the grave is as noble, in its way, as anything in poetry.

> Is there ony room at your head, Saunders?
>     Is there ony room at your feet?
> Or ony room at your side, Saunders,
>     Where fain, fain, I wad sleep?
>
> There's nae room at my head, Marg'ret,
>     There's nae room at my feet;
> My bed it is fu' lowly now,
>     Among the hungry worms I sleep.

In passing, it is interesting to note that an old minstrel ballad, *William and Margaret*, quoted in the *Knight of the Burning Pestle*, and which David Mallet tried to claim for his own, has certain features which suggest it may be a variant of *Clerk Saunders*. Both words and music are given in the appendix to vol. ii of Chappell's *Old English Ditties*.

Obviously, it is almost if not quite impossible to trace the original music to these ancient narratives with any certainty. The difficulties of musical notation hardly troubled the minstrel at all. He carried the tune in his head. Whether he improvised a tune or adapted his improvised verse to an existing tune can never be proved. But the latter is likely to have been the more frequent custom. Not because the minstrel lacked the ability to improvise a tune as readily as a stanza, but in the natural sequence of things the lilt of a well-known tune would be a ready medium for the improvisation of verse. There is plenty of evidence that certain popular tunes were regarded as typical 'ballad-tunes' (e.g. the Castilian *Conde Claros*, the French *L'Abeille*, the Portuguese *Fados*, &c.).[1] The popular English *Jigs* or *Drolls* were farces sung throughout 'to some such tune as *Brave Lord Willoughby*' (*Oxford History of Music*, introd. vol.). Again, in the *Roxburghe Ballads*, which represent the most comprehensive collection of sixteenth- and seventeenth-century ballads in English, each ballad is headed with the name of the tune to which it was sung. Tunes like *Packington's Pound* and *When flying fame* are of frequent occurrence.

With an existing tune as a basis, the formal factors of

[1] Donado in his *Turkish History* speaks of songsters who chanted lyrics set to twenty-four regular tunes, each of which symbolized some particular expression, of joy, grief, love, hate, and so on.

poetic line and metre[1] were already established, and the minstrel was not very much concerned about either variety or subtlety of rhyme. Indeed, his rhyming was nearly always of the simplest, crudest, or most conventional kind.

It is fairly safe to assume that the same tune served for each stanza of the ballad, just as, for example, the twelfth-century plays on the miracles of St. Nicholas consisted of frequent repetitions of the same melody. It would be absurd to look askance at the supposed monotony of this procedure. It was the story that mattered and to its rendering the minstrel could bring all the expressive aids of facial and vocal gesture. Moreover, though to modern ears a folk-melody may seem to be something quaint, it is, in itself, as Fox Strangways has pointed out, a perfectly sincere thing, and 'if we are to get at its real beauty we must do what the singer himself has done, we must sing it all through and many times'.

On the face of it, and there is nothing to contradict it, the ancient ballad must be regarded as a peculiar product of pure minstrelsy. That is to say, it cannot be considered merely as poetry, or as music. Its basis was musical rather than poetical, and the simple factors of its poetry were engendered by a tune. Whether the tune was original or not hardly matters. What does seem to matter is that the poetic process was that of a singer-poet rather than a poet-singer.

In the subsequent discussion of the modern ballad it will be seen that these conclusions have unexpected implications. For the moment they enable us to examine

---

[1] The ballad-quatrain is loose and elastic and with its 'melodious tendency to refrain, was a matter of great importance in the metamorphosis of British verse' (Sir Edmund Gosse).

afresh the usage of the title of ballad for lyric poetry and divers folk-songs even as early as Tudor times. The use of the term may not have been as indiscriminate as it may seem. The creation of a short lyric to fit an existing ballad tune, in place of the lengthy narrative of an earlier epoch, would carry the title by implication. Probably it was from this practice that the fashionable ballad-writing of Tudor and Elizabethan days arose. At the same time the plentiful collection of *Roxburghe Ballads* shows that the rhymed narrative was still popular enough, and these, as has already been said, were all constructed to fit existing popular tunes. Thus, on the one hand, ballad tunes served for lyric poetry, and all kinds of folk-song for narrative poetry, on the other. Inevitably, the title of ballad would become a synonym for anything popular, whether in poetry or music. For, as the age of minstrelsy became more and more remote, the usage of the word would tend to become less definite.

On these grounds, however, the ballad opera would seem to earn its title after all, and the folk-songs which under the title of ballads have come down to us with verbal texts of a purely lyrical character may be, in many cases, the actual tunes to which the ancient minstrel wedded his rhymed story. And in this connexion the concluding paragraph of Fox Strangways's splendid chapter on 'Folk Song' in the introductory volume of the *Oxford History of Music* is significant comment.

The theory that it was a tune which engendered the ancient narrative may lead to a significant understanding of the original choice of the title of ballad. Why should a word so definitely associated with dancing describe a form of narrative poetry? Was it because the minstrel used well-known dance-tunes as the musical medium for his improvisation? It is difficult to resist the simple answer to this question. It would change Percy's generalization—a song accompanied by or accompanying a dance—into a logical definition which would have the merit of taking into account the lexicographical derivation of the word. If we turn again to the definition given on page 4 and add after the word 'stanzas' the significant parenthesis 'which derived their metre and line from the dance-tune to which they were originally sung', it would seem to be quite complete. The folk-ballads, or those narratives which have come down to us associated with certain folk-songs, fit into this definition very conveniently. *Roger de Coverley* is better known as a dance, but there are at least two ballad texts associated with it, namely *Roger de Coverley* and *Arthur O'Bradley*. The eerie narrative of *Widdecombe Fair* is likewise set to a tune which is essentially a dance measure. And the best-known tune of *Barbara Allen* may well have been a minuet or, perhaps, a saraband. 'The names of dances', said Sir Thomas Elyot in 1531, 'were taken, as they be now, either of the names of the first inventors, or of the measure and numbers they do contain, or the first words of the ditty which the song comprehendeth whereof the dance was made.'

However, it is not a safe assumption that the original tune was always a dance-tune. My own memory of a Welsh ballad-monger gives the direct lie to that. For the doggerel version of a mine disaster in a neighbouring valley was sung to the pensive, slow-moving strains of the folk-song *Vale of Clwyd*, while the second story of a county wedding or birth (I forget which) was set to the merry lilt of the *Bells of Aberdovey*.[1] Moreover, the metre

[1] This tune, which the Welsh still claim as a folk-song, is, in reality, a song by Dibdin from his opera, *Liberty Hall* (1785).

of some of the ancient ballads hardly suggests the inspiration of a dance-tune. For general purposes, therefore, the parenthesis already given on page 23 should read 'from the dance-tune or melody to which they were originally sung' if it is to be really acceptable.

By the time selections from these ballad tunes were presented in the guise of ballad opera their identity with narrative poetry had been somewhat obscured. The title of ballad could no longer carry any real distinction of meaning, and soon its use was so perverted and degraded that in 1802 the erudite Dr. Burney could write:

'A ballad is a mean and trifling song such as is generally sung in the streets. In the new French *Encyclopédie* we are told that we English dance and sing our ballads at the same time. We have often heard ballads sung and seen country dances danced; but never at the same time if there was a fiddle to be had. The movement of our country dances is too rapid for the utterance of words. The English ballad has long been detached from dancing, and, since the old translation of the Bible, been confined to a lower order of song.'

The Irish 'tale-teller' never found the reel too fast for his utterance, and the degradation of the ballad has little to do with the translation of the scriptures. Ballad-singing was a popular art, and once it had passed out of the keeping of the minstrels it was almost bound to become more and more indiscriminate. At the same time, the separate arts of poetry and music were destined to fulfil their more studied evolution and distinctive developments.

The musical fundamentals of the ancient ballad were simple enough, and it may seem a comparatively unimportant point to decide whether the tune preceded the words in creation. But, apart from the fact that it may suggest a reason for the original choice of the term 'ballad', there are other questions in the poetic and musical processes which must also be considered. The confusion of ballad tunes with folk-songs is easily understood. Up to the seventeenth century, at least, a ballad tune was a folk-song, as a matter of course, and many folk-songs owed their continued existence to the fact that they were pressed into service as ballad tunes. Very probably the minstrels contributed as much as they owed to their native song, and the confusion therefore is perfectly natural. Misleading though it may be, there is nothing surprising in the fact that one tune is often associated with several texts, or that a single text may be known to several tunes. There is nothing distinctive about a ballad tune, except that it is so often a dance-tune. In short, any discussion of ballad tunes must inevitably stray a good deal through the boundless realm of folk-song generally. But without delving too deeply into the origins and fundamentals of folk-song itself, it will be as well to realize its most significant feature.

Whether the characteristics of folk-song are, as Cecil Gray seems to suggest, mainly international, or, to follow the opinion of Vaughan Williams, they are purely national, or whether, to cite a third case, they are more accurately described as racial, may be open to argument. What is reasonably certain, however, is that a folk-song is essentially practical. It was born to enliven the monotony of a daily task or a tedious march; to mark and elaborate the measure of a dance; or to be the natural medium for the telling of a story or the elaboration of a ceremonial, and its form and style would reflect the need which engendered it. The most casual acquaintance with a collection like the Hebridean Folk-songs, for example, will readily demonstrate this fact. But what does it all imply?

From one point of view, perhaps, Parry in *The Art of Music* has put the matter very concisely. Discussing folk-songs he says:

'A large proportion of the tunes came into existence in connection with poems and ballads which told some story or tragic event of local interest, and each tune was made to fit all the verses, whether they were cheerful or tragical. Such a tune is likely to be little more than a mere design, which might be very pleasant and complete as melodic design in itself, but would leave it to the singer to put in the necessary expression corresponding to the varying sentiment of the words, by giving to a rise in the melody the character of exultant happiness or poignant anguish, and to a fall either reposeful satisfaction or hopeless despair.'

But when the paragraph is examined carefully it may be felt that the questions of the musical process and its performance have not been satisfactorily answered. For example, in an age when these narrative poems were undoubtedly improvised (and not transcribed), would it not seem more feasible to say that all the verses were made to fit a tune rather than the reverse? And again, in the matter of performance, is it enough to say that a rise or fall in the melody must necessarily express such contrasted emotions?

The creation of a tune to fit a number of poetic stanzas is by no means as easy as it may seem. Even the lutenists sometimes failed. Warlock in his discussion on *The English Ayre* writes, 'the composer thought out his melody in such a way that its strong accents fell naturally upon the words demanding stress in the poem (though there were occasional difficulties over second and third verses)'. And it was Brahms who asserted that a strophic song with a single melody for all verses was no lazy device but the supreme accomplishment of the song-writer. It is difficult to believe the minstrel succeeded where the lutenists failed, or that he possessed the intrinsic genius of a Schubert. Moreover, if this were the creative process, the early ballad would have revealed the gradual development of a distinctive form both musically and poetically.

Someone has described folk-song as the pure spring of melody, and nothing could be truer. To overcharge it with emotional subtleties is to destroy its inherent charm of utter simplicity. Born of a practical need and repeated over and over again, it would establish a natural rather than an artificial identity. And wedded to the changing circumstances of varying verbal texts, it would gain elaborations or modifications of the simplest kinds while preserving its intrinsic form and style. Professor Dent[1] has suggested that every quatrain of poetry has the same emotional design, and much the same may be said of every folk-song. In short, it is the simple poetry of melody, fulfilling an instinctive sense of rhythmic design and obeying a natural emotional law.

If for the moment we accept the theory of the tune as a fundamental basis of the ancient ballad, it will be to find a more natural creative process than that suggested by Parry. For the lilt and expression of the tune would inevitably be reflected in the 'improvisation' of each and every stanza, and the metrical and expressive detail of words and music would be instinctively appropriate. This would account, probably, for the fact that almost every ballad betrays a stanzaical pattern in its emotional and expressive outline, and it may also explain the characteristic repetition (or nearly so) of corresponding lines in succeeding stanzas. The aptness of a tune like *The hunt is up* as a basis for the narrative of *Chevy Chase*

[1] *Music & Letters*, October 1936.

is surely quite natural. The fact that at least two other melodies are associated with this ballad would be more significant if we could discover which was the earliest tune.[1]  As it is, it cannot be evidence for either side. And a quotation from Butler's *The Principles of Musicke* (1636) concerning 'the infinite multitude of Ballads set to sundry pleasant and delightful tunes by cunning and witty composers, with country dances fitted unto them' is too ambiguous to prove anything except the connexion of the dance with the ballad.

So it would seem that whether we approach the problem of the ballad from the literary or the musical side we are confronted by the difficulties of unreliable evidence, or, at least, evidence that cannot be safely considered as original. The age of the minstrel has departed for ever. Its activities have come down to us as echoes rather than records of a characteristic social life which we can only realize vaguely.

To regard the narrative ballad as primitive drama or primitive opera is manifestly misleading although, in its own day, it may have fulfilled much the same function. But to consider it as song, in the accepted sense of the word, is almost as ambiguous. The normal definition of song is a melody inspired by poetry. As a phase of art its development is to be traced mainly on musical grounds. We have only to cite the contemporary setting of a poem like *O Mistress Mine* and compare it with the later settings of, say, Sullivan and Quilter to appreciate what this means. Each of the settings would take its place among the songs of its own day quite definitely. But, on musical grounds, how are we to deal with the following versions of the ballad of *Barbara Allan*?

[1] The confusion of texts is an added difficulty. See page 16.

The first is, of course, the familiar tune which cannot be later than the sixteenth century. The verbal text has many variants; that given here is taken from the *Oxford Book of Ballads*.

The Scots air seems to me to be such an apt setting of the words that it might even be the original tune which inspired the narrative. I make no apology for preserving the Scots spelling and expressions. I first heard the tune during the War of 1914–18 at an army concert, and the text represents my honest attempt to transcribe the uncompromising diction of a young Scottish soldier named Murray, with one or two minor alterations.

In Scar-let town where I was born, There was a fair maid dwell-in' Made ev-'ry youth cry Well-a-day. Her name was Bar-b'ra Al-len.

All in the merry month of May
   When green buds they were swellin'
Young Jemmy Grove on his deathbed lay,
   For love of Barb'ra Allen.

He sent his man into her then
   To the town where she was dwellin';
'O haste and come to my master dear
   If your name be Barb'ra Allen.'

So slowly, slowly rase she up,
   And slowly she came nigh him,
And when she drew the curtain by,
   'Young man, I think you're dyin'.'

29

'O its I am sick and very, very sick,
    And it's all for Barb'ra Allen';
'O the better for me ye'se never be
    Tho' your heart's blood were a-spillin'.'

'O dinna ye mind, young man,' says she,
    'When the red wine ye were fillin'
That ye made the healths go round and round,
    And slighted Barb'ra Allen.'

He turned his face unto the wall,
    And death was with him dealin'.
'Adieu, adieu, my dear friends all,
    And be kind to Barb'ra Allen.'

As she was walking o'er the fields
    She heard the dead-bell knellin';
And every jow the dead-bell gave
    Cried 'Woe to Barb'ra Allen'.

'O mother, mother, make my bed,
    O make it soft and narrow;
My love has died for me to-day,
    I'll die for him to-morrow.'

'Farewell,' she said, 'ye virgins all,
    And shun the fault I fell in;
Henceforth take warning by the fall
    Of cruel Barb'ra Allen.'

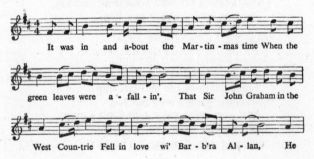

It was in and a-bout the Mar-tin-mas time When the green leaves were a-fall-in', That Sir John Graham in the West Coun-trie Fell in love wi' Bar-b'ra Al-lan, He

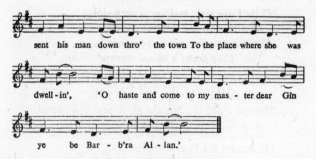

sent his man down thro' the town To the place where she was

dwell-in', 'O haste and come to my mas-ter dear Gin

ye be Bar - b'ra Al - lan.'

O hooly, hooly rase she up
   To the place where he was lyin'
And when she drew the curtain by,
   'Young man, I think ye're dyin'.'
'Its oh, I'm sick, I'm verra, verra sick
   And its a' for Barb'ra Allan.'
'O the better for me ye'se never be
   Tho' your heart's blood were a-spillin'.'

'O dinna ye mind, young man,' she said
   'When the red wine ye were fillin',
That ye made the healths gae round and round
   And slichted Barb'ra Allan.'
He turned his face unto the wa'
   And death was wi' him dealin'.
'Adieu, adieu my dear friends a'
   And be kind to Barb'ra Allan.'

O slowly, slowly rase she up
   And slowly, slowly left him;
And sighing said she couldna stay
   Since death of life had reft him.
She hadna gane a mile but twa
   When she heard the deid-bell knellin',
And ilka jow the deid-bell gaed,
   It cried wae to Barb'ra Allan.

31

'O mither, mither mak my bed,
    And mak' it saft and narrow.
Since my love died for me to-day
    I'll die for him to-morrow.'
'Farewell,' she said, 'ye virgins a'
    And shun the faut I fell in;
Henceforth tak' warning by the fa'
    Of cruel Barb'ra Allan.'

Hooly = softly; slichted = slighted; jow = toll.

But a third version of the same ballad, with more significant verbal changes, is the Dorsetshire tune in five-four
time.

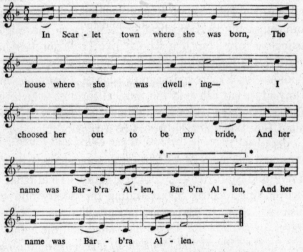

In Scar-let town where she was born, The
house where she was dwell-ing— I
choosed her out to be my bride, And her
name was Bar-b'ra Al-len, Bar b'ra Al-len, And her
name was Bar-b'ra Al-len.

From * to * was probably a unison refrain sung by the audience.

Whether the rhythmic subtleties of this tune were
original, or arose, quite naturally, in the process of fitting
the words to it must be a matter for conjecture. The
elongation of the accented crotchets here and there
would bring it into compound duple time and a recog-

nizable dance rhythm. It is dangerous, perhaps, to assume too much in considering the way in which a tune like this was evolved, and only the discovery of an earlier version in typical dance form would prove my suggestion. Folksong is begotten, not made; begotten of a long succession of singers altering, extending, elaborating, and corrupting. It is a natural growth over a long period of years, an evolutionary process of many minds.

It is obvious that the ballad in music, as in poetry, fully justifies Earle Welby's remark quoted on page 4, which might easily be rewritten 'Ballad does not differ from ballad as a song by Purcell differs from one by Sullivan', and so on. This would almost suggest that the ballad, both musically and poetically, possesses a thoroughly distinctive form, but if a scholar like Professor Ker had to evade the issue with regard to the poetry it would be invidious for a mere musician to suggest a formula; and if any musician can find the musical formula which will express the three tunes just quoted and the many other ballad tunes available, it would be a remarkable feat, to say the least.

It is not the form of the early ballad which matters, but its style and character as a complete entity. To attempt to discover this identity by separating the poetry and the music will lead to the wildest contradictions. Robert Graves, in *The English Ballad*, has stated that the ballad is 'incomplete without music, *music of a repetitive kind that excites and sustains*'. Subsequently the author enlarges on this point, but it is doubtful whether the musician is much clearer even then. How far can the remark be applied to either of the foregoing examples, and how far does it go towards defining any general characteristics in the music of all ballads? Mr. Graves is too much influenced, perhaps, by the theory of communal authorship, and tends to overstress the importance of the 'cumulative' ballads like *The first day of Christmas*, *Who killed Cock Robin?*, &c.

Even if one could believe that a group-mind could evolve a narrative poem, it would be stretching coincidence a little too far to suppose that they would also evolve a tune. And though the basis of a prevailing popular melody be admitted, it only affirms the musical origins of the ballad, and so brings us back to a discussion of folk-song. Thus, if the ballad is 'incomplete without music', the music was complete enough without the poem. Although, in some respects, the communal ballad which is usually 'cumulative' in style may be, as Mr. Graves thinks, one of the earliest manifestations of the ballad, I am more inclined to think it represents a species of performance rather than a characteristic origin. It does not belong to a particular age, but has persisted in different ways down to the present day. The War of 1914–18 was responsible for many of these cumulative songs, and whilst they may have had a communal authorship it is significant that they are always crude, and generally set, most inappropriately, to religious or sentimental tunes. Perhaps they partake of the art of parody as much as the art of the ballad. Incidentally, the sea-ballads, *chanties*, and *forebitters* offer a clue to the land ballads. The *chanty* was a 'ballad of work'—in other words, the slow evolution of a tune to the rhythm of a task, and the setting of a crude versification to its lilt. The *forebitters*, on the other hand, were an affair of solo and chorus, or the alternation of narrative and refrain, the former relying on the improvisation of a soloist, while the chorus was anything from the repetition of a rhythmical set of meaningless syllables to the very apt repetition of a particular sentence. We see much the same process in a ballad like *Widdecombe Fair* of course, and in a lesser degree, in the use of a refrain in some of the minstrel ballads, as in *The Milldams of Binnorie*, for example.

But in general, the early ballad is not defined so conveniently. Undoubtedly, it can only be realized as a peculiar manifestation of folk-song, and shares with folk-song that paradoxical quality of being a thoroughly distinctive product while defying exact definition. It is significant that in the modern art-ballad we shall find that the element of folk-song is a notable characteristic.

It only remains to point out a few of the musical characteristics of these early ballads. It is true to say that the ballad tunes are not so impressed with modal influences as many of our native folk-songs; or it may be that the predominance of the Dorian and Ionian modes in English folk-song is most definitely noticeable in these old ballad tunes. The Ionian mode is, of course, the same as our modern major scale, and in the sixteenth century its popularity with the ballad-mongers earned the disdain of the skilled musicians who deemed it *il modo lascivo*, never dreaming it was destined to survive and be the basis of modern music. The Dorian mode, on the other hand, has a certain affinity with our minor scale. Thus the tonality of these ballad tunes hardly ever suggests any archaic quality to the modern ear; moreover, many of them, no doubt, have been so modified by succeeding generations that all traces of modal influences have been quite destroyed. Rhythmically, the impress of the dance is probably the most important influence. The even measure of four-bar phrases is fairly common, although the three-bar phrase is generally characteristic of the livelier tunes, or those derived from jig and hornpipe tunes. Again, the feeling if not the notation of compound-time is quite noticeable in the seventeenth century and is the result of French influences. It is noteworthy, too, that ballads in the minor key have a definite sugges-tion of the relative major in the second half of the tune, as in the Scots air quoted on page 30, while major key ballads almost invariably have the half close on the dominant. The purely national elements which distinguish Irish, Scottish, Welsh, and English tunes need not be discussed here. The remarks of Mr. Graves, in the work already cited, can be applied, in some degree, to the music as to the poetry. Often, too, the melodic and rhythmic lineaments of a tune will betray a certain instrumental influence, as, for example, in the 'harp-melodies' of the Irish and Welsh, and so on. Lastly, it may be that because a folk-song was evolved by endless repetition, it bears repetition so much better than the creative efforts of later composers. At all events, the ballad tunes had to bear such repetition and did so, very successfully.

Perhaps I may be pardoned for a brief digression here, in order to defend my own country's melodies against the faint praise of so distinguished a scholar as Dr. Ernest Walker. 'Considerably the least artistically interesting of the four large departments of British folk-music', he writes, 'is that contributed by the Welsh people.'[1] When it was written (in 1907) there was, perhaps, some justifica-tion for the remark. Brinley Richards was not a Villiers Stanford, and it was not until the founding of the Welsh Folk Song Society by Dr. Lloyd Williams in 1908 that the true merit of Welsh melody could begin to be revealed. The Victorian collections had few tunes which did not

[1] Ernest Walker, *History of Music in England* (O.U.P.).

betray the chordal elements of 'harp melodies'. Moreover, there were too many traces of indiscriminate editing. But the energy and scholarship of Dr. Lloyd Williams and later disciples have discovered a considerable store of lovely melodies which are a 'joy to the singer'. These melodies show a variety, a melodic flexibility, and an expressive subtlety not to be found in the more circumscribed harp melodies erroneously regarded as typical of Welsh music. Dr. Walker has said that the characteristic features of Welsh music show 'a fondness for triple time, an avoidance of rhythmical organization save of the very simplest nature, an emotional expressiveness of a direct and slightly heavy kind, a certain monotony of invention'; furthermore that there are 'hardly any examples of modal melodies'. The prevalence of triple time is true, although exceptions are plentiful, such as *Yr Hufen Melyn*, *Yn Nyffryn Clwyd*, and *Y Bore Glas*. The remaining statements can hardly be sustained in the face of these later researches. Modal influences are implicit in the Dorian flavour of the Welsh 'Hwyl'. In Jane Williams's collection (1844) 'nearly a fifth of the airs are clearly in the ancient modes, and yet the wrong signatures prefixed to them show that the collector was under the impression that they were some peculiar modification of the minor mode'.[1] The Methodist Revival was a mixed blessing for Welsh folk-music, especially for the old dance-tunes. The domination of the hymn-tune was definitely established. However, the modal flavour of many of the Alawon Gymreig derived from native airs is a very significant feature. In short, since 1908 it seems to be evident that Welsh folk-music is not so very inferior to the rest of the British Isles, and the fact that Dr. Walker makes no men-

[1] Lloyd Williams and Somervell, Introd. to *Welsh Melodies* (Boosey).

tion of these points in the appendix to his second edition (1924) must be my excuse for doing so here.

Mr. Graves has found it possible to trace the succession of the ballad in poetry from its local or folk-lore origins down to its later cultural manifestation, the literary epic. He gives Tennyson's *Idylls of the King* as an example and traces it back to Malory's *Morte d'Arthur*, a prose romance which itself was probably derived from an earlier ballad cycle. The succession of the ballad in music may not follow so direct a path, but it is to be discovered nevertheless. Whether or not it is agreed that the fundamentals of the early ballad were musical, it cannot be denied that the poetic influences flowed quite naturally into the subsequent stream of poetic progress, while the music inevitably maintained the aloofness of folk-song from the subsequent development of music as a creative art. The ballad tune became a factor in ballad opera only to lose its identity therein. And the ballads of the eighteenth and nineteenth centuries followed the broad highway which led to the 'royalty ballad' and the sentimental drawing-room song. The modern ballad, on the other hand, fulfilled its higher destiny, and as will be seen, it did so by realizing in part some of the characteristics of its ancient original.

The ballad opera may seem a far cry from the old minstrel ballad. Both, of course, were popular entertainment, but there the likeness seems to end. Some of us may see some significance in the fact that, at first, lyrics were fitted to existing music. These tunes were ballad airs of varying antiquity. Later, dance-tunes by composers like Purcell, Handel, Corelli, the Scarlattis, were requisitioned, and when the 'surface strata of folk-song had been apparently exhausted', musical numbers by contemporary composers were commissioned. The ballad opera enjoyed two distinct periods of popularity, from 1725 to about 1735, and from 1762 until it lost its identity with ballad tunes and became a species of comic opera. It was an English ballad opera, Coffey's *The Devil to pay* (1728), produced in Germany under the title of *Der Teufel ist los*, which helped to establish the *Singspiel* tradition of that country. In the main, the ballad opera depended on pure satire for its appeal, although the earliest example was *The Gentle Shepherd* of Allan Ramsay, a pastoral play with lyrics adapted to old Scottish tunes. And it has been said that Gay was inspired to write *The Beggar's Opera* because of Swift's remark that 'a Newgate pastoral might make an odd pretty sort of thing'. It is only in its earlier examples, however, that the ballad opera possesses any connexion with the ballad as we are considering it now. Its subsequent development was only anticipating a type of operatic production which has always been popular in England.

The next step is towards the creations of a composer like Dibdin, and the advent of the popular song was inevitable. But not immediately, for traditional ballads like *The Vicar of Bray* (generally dated 1720) and *A hunting we will go*, a traditional air happily wedded to Fielding's words, about twenty years later, are definitely in the line of succession to the old ballads.[1] But the efforts of the composers, with only a few honourable exceptions, rarely get beyond a dismal mediocrity. It must not be forgotten, however, that the social life of the century was far different from the conditions under which the early ballads were

[1] See also *A Ballad*, by George Mason and John Earsden, the fifth of the 'Ayres that were sung and played at Brougham Castle in Westmorland, in the King's Entertainment: Given by the Right Honourable the Earle of Cumberland and his Right Noble Sonne the Lord Clifford, 1618'.

created. Moreover, it was a time when English music was indifferent in quality, and lacking in individuality.

It is hardly surprising that, having 'taken the stage' in the ballad opera, the ballad should find its subsequent composers among musicians who were all associated with the theatre. Arne, Leveridge, Dibdin, Hook, Shield, Percy, Davy, and Braham were all stage composers, and many of their ballads are taken from dramatic productions. Arne had enough genius to have produced some really characteristic songs. Perhaps his best song is the setting of Shakespeare's *Come away, Death*, but his ballads, like *Despairing beside a clear stream*, have a shallow prettiness, or, like *The Miller of Mansfield*, a melodious self-consciousness which is out of keeping with the traditional style. Leveridge, on the other hand, with but a fraction of Arne's talent, could produce a song like *The Roast Beef of Old England*, which has become almost a traditional air. His ballads, like *All in the Downs* and *Black-eyed Susan*, also have very distinct merits. It has been said that many of his songs, which he published in 1720, are adaptations from Irish traditional airs. Be that as it may, there is a characteristic style about his melodies which has something of the flavour of the traditional ballad tunes. Dibdin's name is always associated with sea songs. He was not a polished composer, but he had all the versatility of a real trouper and a facility which came of a quick wit and a varied practical experience. His *Tom Bowling* and *The Jolly Young Waterman* are admirable ballads. Other examples, like *Ben Backstay*, *The Lamplighter*, and *I sailed from the Downs in the Nancy*, are of less merit, perhaps, although they all have a certain individuality about them. Almost all his ballads are taken from his dramatic works and 'table entertainments'.

For example, all the above, except one, were included in *The Oddities*, which was produced at the Lyceum in 1789. James Hook was an artistic composer with a certain daintiness of style, and despite its prettiness there is the right quality in his ballad *The Lass of Richmond Hill*. Shield must be included here for his *Death of Tom Moody*, although few would wish to perpetuate his song *The Wolf*. Yet, in some ways, Shield was the most gifted composer of them all. Percy, of course, is remembered for his *Wapping Old Stairs* and John Davy for his *Bay of Biscay*, both of which are typical ballads of their day. Finally, we have the remarkable Braham, the celebrated tenor singer, whose ballad *The Death of Nelson* comes from the opera *The American*, produced in 1811.

This has brought us to the beginning of the nineteenth century, and so to the threshold of the Victorian age. Looking back over the list I have just surveyed it may be remarked, with truth, that the influence of the *chanty* is far more predominant than that of the traditional ballad. But these eighteenth-century ballads were the products of their age and come mainly from stage productions which were highly artificial in style and character. The melodies lack the simple fluency of the early traditional tunes, and are either too self-conscious or over-dramatic. The true element of narrative, too, is often missing, as might be expected in an age when wit was preferred to romance. One of the features of the ancient ballad was its remarkable fusion of the simple and heroic in tragedy. In the eighteenth century tragedy was neither simple nor heroic, but often both sordid and mean. Moreover, there is to be felt a certain quality of pettiness, even using the word in its best sense, which limited the vision and set the horizon of literary imagination within the narrow angle of rationalism. In temper and taste there was a lack of the very qualities which had engendered the ancient ballad, and its eclipse was inevitable. The limelight of the theatre was no just exchange for the pure sunlight of native song or the natural impulse of minstrelsy. But worse was to come. The banalities of the Victorian ballad, however, must be left for a later chapter.

To recapitulate, I cannot do better than compile a list of the principal features of the early ballad in music to be taken in conjunction with that given by Mr. Graves in *The English Ballad*.

1. The early ballad has no known author or composer.
2. There can be no authoritative text of an early ballad.
3. It is primarily a product of minstrelsy.
4. It was a poetic improvisation based on a tune, which was often but not always a dance-tune.
5. It was meant for performance rather than posterity.
6. It can only be regarded as a particular manifestation of folk-song.
7. After the days of minstrelsy, it tends to become confused with folk-song generally.
8. Apart from the individual essays of the minstrels there are those ballads which are communal in origin and performance. Nearly all of the cumulative songs are probably to be considered in this category.
9. It is obvious that the musical attributes of the early ballad are precisely those of folk-song itself.

It is not unlikely that other features could find their place in this summary, but these are, perhaps, the main lines of argument which I have advanced. As to the succession of the ballad in music, we have only reached that point where the tunes lost their original identity in the ballad opera and thereafter gained only a doubtful imitation in the examples of stage composers, who were more impressed by the sea-shanty than the ancient narrative ballad, which, for all its crudities, exercised a profound influence on our national literature and served to perpetuate some of our loveliest tunes.

A word must be said about American traditional ballads. Mr. Theodore Roosevelt once wrote to Lomax, the compiler of *American Ballads and Folk Songs* and similar collections, 'there is something very interesting in the reproduction here on this new continent of essentially the conditions of ballad-growth which obtained in medieval England; including, by the way, sympathy for the outlaw Jesse James taking the place of Robin Hood'. The folk-songs of the Appalachians retain very distinctive marks of the Old World from whence they came, particularly in the music. And the indisputable fact that a great many of the American ballads—those 'death bed confession pieces, songs of local murders and disasters . . . of faithless lovers . . .' and the like—are set to Irish melodies, to hymn-tunes, and popular songs is very significant. For it follows that process of the tune inspiring the words which I have already suggested.

It only remains to refer the reader to the many collections of ballads enumerated at the end of the book. To have included even a few examples of the ancient ballad in the foregoing pages would have involved several music pages and the discussion of the many variants in tune and text and their origins. These matters are more effectively dealt with in those collections entirely devoted to such music. No doubt the student will find it interesting to test my arguments by his own personal research. He may safely be promised the discovery of some gems of native song as a delightful reward.

## CHAPTER III
## MODERN BALLADS

ONCE the ballad[1] takes it place among modern song forms it is compelled to face the severest analysis. Luckily, among its sponsors are some of the greatest song writers in the world. Its avowed originator, in Germany at least, was Carl Loewe. It is possible he may have suffered a little of the obscurity which attaches to every pioneer. It is equally possible that in an age of strong personalities he lacked a certain forcefulness in his music. At all events, opinions about him are sharply divided. A critic like Dannreuther could damn him with faint praise; a singer like Henschel could exalt him to a place beside his famous contemporary Schubert. Later we may discover some definite reasons for these extreme opinions. Loewe apart, however, the names of Schubert, Schumann, Brahms, Liszt, Wagner, and Wolf are a sufficient indication that the song-narrative has a very distinguished place in the history of the *lied*. The distinctive work of the Russians and also of the Czechs is of considerable importance. And we shall find that English song is not without its representation.

A brief review of the most notable examples of the modern ballad is obviously necessary before any general criticism can be undertaken. Before doing so, it may be as well to consider the limits of the review. It will obviously be indicative rather than exhaustive. But when so able a critic as Dannreuther allows the title of ballad for Liszt's *Die Drei Zigeuner* while he describes the same composer's

[1] The English spelling is preserved throughout to avoid confusion with the French ballade.

*Die Lorelei* as a scena, it is easy to see there are difficulties ahead. From one point of view he is quite justified in distinguishing these two songs. They are different. But whether the modern ballad is to be so rigidly circumscribed is open to argument.

However, if we take some ninety or more examples (ranging over German ballads from Loewe to Pfitzner and including, too, the contemporary work of composers like Schreker, Křenek, and Weill; Russian ballads from Glinka to the younger Tcherepnin; as well as representative examples from Britain, France, Czechoslovakia, the Scandinavian countries, &c.) it should be possible to form some notion of the common artistic ideals which lie behind this particular phase of song. Incidentally, examples like *Senta's Ballad* and *Varlaam's Ballad* are not to be excluded because they are taken from operas. In some cases I have deemed it advisable to consider settings of the same poem by different composers, e.g. *Erlkönig* by Loewe and Schubert, *Die Beiden Grenadiere* by Wagner and Schumann, *Der Sänger* by Loewe, Schubert, Schumann, and Wolf, and so on. Comparative criticism of this sort has its disadvantages, it is true, but is not without significance in the present instances.

Before passing on to the critical analysis of the music there are some important preliminary observations to be made with reference to the poetic ideals which lay behind this renaissance of the ballad, and the changed conditions in the creative process. Moreover, the nineteenth century was one of almost unexampled activity in the art of music generally, and that of song particularly; and no phase of the art could escape the influences of the distinctive developments in music-drama, and the progress of instrumental (in this case, especially pianoforte) technique.

And the later tendencies in the direction of programme music are not to be ignored.

Apart from the obvious fact that the renaissance of the ballad is an indication of the poetic reaction against classicism, it is also a signpost on the road to romanticism. It is interesting to note that Goethe considered the ballad should always have 'a tone of awe-inspiring mystery, which fills the reader's mind with the presence of supernatural powers, and contain strong dramatic elements'. Again, there is to be noted that tendency to bring the narrative nearer to the lyrical ideal in the *Romanze*.

The creative process must now fall into line with that impulse which inclined song writers to greater refinements in the ideal of correct declamation in the setting of words to music, an impulse which runs through the history of the *lied* from the spontaneous Schubert to the immaculate Wolf. The progress in pianoforte technique brings to mind the important work of Schumann and Liszt, and, finally, the influence of Wagner must loom large in those examples which belong to the latter half of the century. At the same time, this is no place to anticipate the conclusions which should, more properly, come after the consideration of the musical examples; but when a composer like Schubert has completed his work before the birth of Brahms while his contemporary, Loewe, can furnish examples as far apart as 1818 and 1857, it is as well to keep in mind these factors in the musical progress.

It may seem scant justice not to mention the ballads of Zumsteeg, Zelter, and Reichardt, who were, undoubtedly, the pioneers in this phase of the *lied*. In general terms, however, their work was too unequal, and hardly distinctive enough to suggest the foundations of a significant art form for the modern ballad. I begin, therefore, with Carl Loewe, although *Erlkönig*, one of his earliest ballads, is three years later than Schubert's masterpiece of 1815. Loewe's claim to fame rests solely on his ballads, and perhaps his first, *Edward*,[1] is also his finest example. Dialogue narrative offers a definite advantage in the matter of musical form, and Loewe succeeds in giving a distinct identity to both characters in this ballad. Word painting is simply but superbly achieved, and the expressive pianoforte part, never ornate but always vivid, maintains the dramatic tension admirably. The musical detail fulfils all the psychological changes in the narrative, and the form is adroitly fashioned out of the inevitable sequence in the dramatic situation. The bare harmonies of Edward's first words, the dramatic lift of the vocal line (above the same basic harmonies) for his second reply, the growing apprehension of the mother, the vivid modulation for the son's terrible confession, the gathering speed of the drama down to the last dreadful curse, are all accomplished with an astonishing musical economy and with a masterly conciseness of form. For it will be noted that the contrasted themes associated with each of the two characters obtain their distinctive developments within the dramatic scheme, and, at the end, it is the mother's theme which rightly returns in effect, though with heightened poignancy and terror, while Edward's awful curse (a masterly example of dramatic declamation), being so far removed from his earlier equivocations, is derived, musically, from his true confession and furnishes a fitting and vivid climax to a work of sheer genius. The rhythmic subtleties and the expressive dramatic poise and variety of the recurring 'O' of the poem are further evidences of

[1] Cf. settings of this poem by Adolf Jensen, op. 58, no. 3, and Tchaikovsky (to a translation by Tolstoy), op. 46, no. 2.

the composer's sense of dramatic detail. *Edward* can surely be offered as an outstanding example of the dramatic and musical attributes of the true art ballad.

Loewe's other ballads, with the exception of *Erlkönig* which will later be considered with Schubert's setting, hardly reach the magnificent heights of *Edward*. They reveal a composer who lacked sufficient self-criticism to make his evident search for a musical formula of the art ballad uniformly successful. His musical inspiration was not always spontaneous enough. At the same time, his ballads generally demonstrate the value of certain musical characteristics in giving unity and eloquence to the narrative as a whole. *Herr Olaf*, written in 1821, has the merit of thematic economy and dramatic continuity, although the climax does not touch the vivid heights of the former ballad. The opening vocal phrase, derived from the bass of the pianoforte prelude, is characteristic enough, and effective use is made of the subsequent vocal melody of some six bars as a basis for the first four stanzas. After a momentary and fitting return to the opening motif, the music changes with the change of scene. Again it is a short pregnant phrase which holds the stage until the hint of the coming wedding pomp, after which we come to the last tragic climax, which has a quiet effectiveness of its own. *Der Wirthin Töchterlein* (1823) is fashioned, very effectively, out of folk-song and simple dramatic declamation. Thematically, the whole song is evolved from the melody of the first line. Unfortunately, the song ends with a somewhat commonplace and unnecessary pianoforte arpeggio. Again it is folk-song which is the musical basis of the excellent *Heinrich der Vogler*, written in 1836. But when we turn to his *Archibald Douglas* (1857) it is to find a strange amalgam of folk-song and

Wagner's *Flying Dutchman*. The opening phrase of the pianoforte prelude is found to have an unexpected significance as the story is unfolded, and on that tiny motif and the first eight bars of the vocal melody the whole of the rather lengthy ballad is virtually founded. There are some effective touches in the accompaniment, and the whole work has an undoubted musical unity and a splendid sense of dramatic poise.

It would seem that the musical characteristics which Loewe tried to establish for the modern ballad were the impress of folk-song, the accomplishment of artistic unity by evolving the whole work from a short and distinctive theme (or themes) capable of development in accordance with the dramatic demands of the narrative, while the accompaniment furnished all the descriptive detail. Here then is an acknowledgement of the folk-lore basis of the ballad, the foundations of a musical form which is both logical and fluent, and, finally, an artistic reality for the pianoforte accompaniment in fulfilling at once the musical and dramatic needs of the scheme. Singers will always admire Loewe for a vocal line which maintains a melodious continuity despite the declamatory requirements; and if his piano writing lacks the skill of a Schumann or a Liszt, his ideals with regard to the accompaniment are undoubtedly significant.

Because of these virtues, Loewe's *Erlkönig* will always bear comparison with Schubert's setting. It is generally believed that Loewe was unacquainted with the earlier song of his great contemporary. There is no doubt that, in their different ways, both songs are masterpieces, and Tovey's masterly comparison of them can hardly be bettered.[1] The Schubert is a divine inspiration which

[1] Essay on Schubert: *Heritage of Music*, vol. i.

49

goes straight to the heart of the poem to discover that the dramatic pulse is the mad gallop in action and the child's terror in feeling. Loewe's is a more rationalistic conception, and by comparison his realism is more theatrically achieved. But it is excellent 'theatre', and a ballad is none the worse for that. The way of the Schubert is the way of a rare genius. It is not a model; it is a miracle. The Loewe, on the other hand, will stand beside his *Edward* as perfect examples of a significant and truly eloquent art form.

Schubert's extraordinary ballad *Der Zwerg* (1823) fully justifies Richard Capell's high praise and is, in my opinion, a vindication of Loewe's method. 'Here', says Capell, 'was the foundation of something very like Wagner's melodious declamation.' The whole ballad is evolved from two short themes, the first reminiscent of the 'fate' motif in Beethoven's C minor Symphony; the second a short descending phrase. Capell rightly describes the poem as 'insufferable nonsense', but the music obtains a remarkable unity and vividness with an astonishing thematic economy. *Der Fischer* (1815) is a simple strophic song. It has all the quiet charm of folk-song. The narrative is not in the music, but it will need to be in the singing. Perhaps another quotation from Capell will be significant here. 'The wandering minstrels whose art has survived only in folklore must have composed like this. Yes, in Schubert we have a specimen of an elusive race, a folk-song composer, pinned down for once and documented!'[1] As an example of a dialogue ballad, *Der Tod und das Mädchen* (1817) comes readily to the mind.

But the art of Schubert often defies the analyst. A genius who could so spontaneously wed a *Ländler* to a

[1] Richard Capell, *Schubert's Songs* (Benn).

Shakespearian lyric, and re-echo the popular music of his day in many a master-song, could be expected to react to the ballad in a variety of ways. When, as in *Hagars Klage*, or *Der Taucher* or *Die Bürgschaft* or *Ritter Toggenburg*,[1] he was following the method of Zumsteeg, unity was often lost even though there were lovely fragments to be found here and there. The unfinished *Johanna Sebus* sets us wondering what might have been, but then the strophic *Der Schatzgräber* or *Der Gott und die Bajadere* may disappoint us. And *Der Sänger* is, for our present purpose, more interesting when compared with the settings of Loewe, Schumann, and Wolf.

Schubert was undoubtedly the greatest lyricist in the history of song, and, as Capell says, 'few of his poets wrote narrative ballads quite as naturally as he wrote tunes'. But it is the disciple of Zumsteeg and not Schubert who disappoints us, and, even then, being Schubert, he charms us. After all, his lyricism did open magic casements in all the musical forms, and in song it could embrace an astonishing variety from the dainty *Heidenröslein* to the stark *Doppelgänger*. Few of his poets could have written a more indifferent ballad than Collin's *Der Zwerg*, and that Schubert translated into a masterpiece.

Perhaps singers are inclined to regard the strophic song as an easy song, which is a gross mistake; and in the case of a narrative song, a grievous misjudgement. For we have seen that the ancient ballad was a poetic improvisation set to a simple strophic melody with all the descriptive and dramatic lineaments expressed in the art of performance. The modern ballad set in simple strophic style

[1] Perhaps the cantata-like *Einsamkeit* (Mayrhofer) should be noted here. It should not be confused with the song of the same title from the *Winterreise*.

would seem then to demand far more of the singer than that written in *durchcomponirt* style, and, from another angle, it is as true to say it demands a music which will compare with the spontaneous Schubertian melody or the indefinable fluency of folk-song. Above all, it must be realized that the terms 'strophic' and *durchcomponirt* do not describe song forms but rather methods of song writing, a fact which is much more important than it may seem.

When we come to the consideration of Schumann, the tendency to associate the ballad form with that of the *Romanze* is unmistakable. *Belshazzar*, *Die Löwenbraut*, and *Die Beiden Grenadiere* are without doubt his best examples, and, happily for the present purpose, are distinctive in form and character. *Die Löwenbraut* is the nearest to the Loewe tradition, the whole song being evolved, virtually, from the opening pianoforte phrase and the first four bars of the vocal melody. The narrative gains its detail from a fluent and vivid pianoforte accompaniment, and the vocal line maintains a characteristic fluency in declamation and expression. Like most of Schumann's music it is suggestive rather than graphic in effect, but it has a splendid dramatic continuity and is a ballad which deserves to be better known than it is. *Belshazzar*, the best of the three examples, is more lyrical in style, although it succeeds in being the most dramatic in effect. Much of this is due to the superb pianoforte accompaniment. The structural elements of the song are the four clearly defined musical strophes, the third of which begins in the subdominant and ends in the dominant, while the other three begin and end in the tonic. But though the formal unity of the ballad is established by these arbitrary musical means rather than the dramatic exigencies of the narrative, there is little doubt that

Schumann has succeeded in portraying the three dramatic essentials of the poem—the noisy banquet scene, the inexplicable writing, and the death of Belshazzar—in a most vivid manner. Altogether this is by far the most satisfying of Schumann's ballads, and English singers should take advantage of an excellent translation which is now available.[1] *Die Beiden Grenadiere*, one of his most popular songs, betrays the impress of folk-song and is typical Schumann in form and style. Aided again by an excellent pianoforte accompaniment and a superb declamation, the melodic continuity leads with an inevitable sureness to the effective introduction of the *Marseillaise* for a striking climax, although there is something incongruous in the fact that 'two Napoleonic soldiers should express their ardent devotion to the Emperor to the strains of the most republican of songs'.[2] But then the same notion had occurred to Wagner, although in his case it is not drawn into the vocal line but is kept to the pianoforte accompaniment. Unfortunately, Wagner's setting was made to a . French translation (by Loeve-Veimars) which is so different from Heine's rhythm that the original German will not fit the music at all. Posterity has decided quite rightly that Schumann's is the better setting, although the Wagner is not without its fine moments. In style and date it belongs to his *Rienzi* and *Flying Dutchman* period. Most of Wagner's songs were 'chippings' from his workshop during the creation of his mighty operatic works, and another ballad, *Der Tannenbaum*, written in Riga in 1839, reflects the style of the music of *Tannhäuser*.

But it is *Senta's Ballad* which is to be cited as his most characteristic example, and the composer's undisguised

[1] By Samuel Langford (O.U.P.).
[2] Eric Blom: *Step-children of Music* (Foulis).

admiration for Loewe's work is a sufficient indication of his regard for the ballad as an art form. In its formal aspect, therefore, it is not surprising that *Senta's Ballad* reflects the Loewe tradition. But there are other considerations which are very important. First of all, the dramatic situation is unique. For here is a narrative which forms a dramatic unit within the unfolding of the very same story. The ballad is the story of the opera, and the opera the dramatic presentation of the ballad.

It is an interesting fact that the *Flying Dutchman* was intended originally to be a dramatic ballad in one act, and in the opinion of Dannreuther 'the division into three acts is made by means of crude cuts, and new starts equally crude'. Be that as it may, the thematic content of the whole opera is considerably indebted to that of *Senta's Ballad* itself. It is important to remember, too, that Wagner's vocal writing shows very distinct changes during the course of his creative career. There was a period when he seemed to aim at a purely vocal effectiveness in his melodies. Later, in the *Flying Dutchman* and in *Tannhäuser* for example, the vocal melody is more definitely related to, and regulated by, the dramatic action. And in the final stage of development the vocal line tends to be more independent of the musical texture as a whole, being, in effect, an intensified declamation of the words themselves.

The vocal melody of *Senta's Ballad* is certainly born of the dramatic expression of the narrative. The two themes (which, appropriately enough, begin and end the opera itself) have been described by Kobbé[1] as the Ocean and Senta motifs. Whatever the 'labels', and there have been many, the thematic purpose is readily apparent, and

[1] Kobbé, *Complete Opera Book* (Putnam, 1925).

it is a striking dramatic unity which gives the descending chromatic scale of the opening instrumental bars to the final climax of Senta's utterance. The vocal line throughout affords the singer every opportunity of vivid and expressive declamation, although the melody preserves a comparative simplicity in rhythm and outline. Beneath it the colourful and descriptive orchestral texture serves to point the narrative and to enhance its dramatic effect. It is perhaps idle to speculate as to what might have resulted had Wagner maintained his original intention of presenting the work as a dramatic ballad in one act.[1] He did not do so, and his original ideals are only a matter for conjecture. As it was, he gave us a ballad complete in itself within a dramatic framework which was an expansion of this smaller unit. What is significant is that he was alive to the dramatic possibilities of the ballad, and in the light of later developments in the modern ballad that fact is important.

Liszt's contributions to the modern ballad are as varied and unequal in style and in merit as are his songs in general. His was a remarkable talent, so often astonishingly daring and original, and as often prone to be somewhat commonplace. The Schiller ballads, *Der Fischerknabe* and *Der Alpenjäger*, as well as the Uhland *Die Vätergruft*, are more or less in the Loewe tradition without being very striking examples. The Goethe *Es war ein König in Thule* suffers by comparison with the settings by Berlioz and by Gounod; mainly because, as in so many of his songs, Liszt is guilty of over-emphasis. Even his finest ballad (and perhaps his most characteristic song), *Die Drei Zigeuner*, is not entirely free from this fault, but there the effect seems more natural and, in some ways,

[1] It is sometimes performed in this way.

more in keeping with the poetic atmosphere. The popular and effective *Die Lorelei* is certainly in the style of an operatic scena, but with a closer thematic unity. In many ways it foreshadows the dramatic ballad of the later Russians. Moreover, it compels the consideration of an artistic problem with which the modern ballad was bound to be confronted.

There must always be a curious duality in a poetic narrative. Lyrical and stanzaical in form, it is, nearly always, dramatic in effect. Composers, like Schumann and Brahms for example, who were impressed with the lyrical form tended to bring it nearer the ideal of the *Romanze*. Others were ready to exploit its dramatic possibilities and so to enlarge its scope and style. Obviously there must be artistic limits on both sides, and the poetic context should be the deciding factor always.

So before passing on to Brahms, who maintains most consistently and successfully the lyrical ideal, it may be as well to consider the comments of Dannreuther in his criticism of Loewe.[1]

'Declamation, histrionic changes of voice, and even mimicry are called upon to bear their part. With the aid of the musical actor's art some of Loewe's *Balladen* . . . are effective enough, but they need such external assistance to cover defects in the music. The poetry usually is allowed to tell its own story, but the music is subordinate. There is a sense of insecurity. Rarely does the musical mood embrace the entire poem, and almost invariably the stress is laid upon the externals of the story rather than upon the lyrical emotion which underlies it. The impression left is that of a partially musical recitation by an actor, not the consistent outpouring of a musician.'

Those remarks deserve close scrutiny, and that is my excuse for quoting so fully. At first sight it seems that

[1] *Oxford History of Music*, vol. vi.

Dannreuther is not impressed with the ballad as a distinctive art form. At the same time, his denial of the title for *Die Lorelei* implies that he recognized the distinctive elements of Loewe's work. But if the modern ballad is to be a logical (though more sophisticated) development of the ancient, some of his strictures are not so sweeping as they may seem. In the ancient ballad, although the music may have been the basis for the purely formal elements of the poetry, it was certainly subordinate to it in the matter of performance. The repetition of a tune for verse after verse of varying sentiments suggests that such a tune could only be a simple musical design. And lovely though it often was, it could only be a convenient medium for the telling of a story, and not the definitive expression of the story itself. The histrionic abilities of the minstrel were obviously needed to carry the narrative into effective performance. It is a little difficult to see where the insecurity of Loewe's music is revealed. Admittedly it had its defects at times, but the small thematic range achieved a sense of unity by the simplest means.

The opening of *Die Lorelei* immediately suggests the operatic recitative, an effect which is not to be found in Loewe. Nor in such as *Senta's Ballad*, where it might have been appropriate enough. Thus, Dannreuther's last sentence loses its significance. It is one thing to set a dramatic text to a melody which is simple enough in rhythm, outline, and development to permit the singer every chance for effective dramatic declamation, and quite another to set the text to a musical recitative which is distinctly declamatory in style and feature. Which of the two is more likely to leave the impression of 'a partially musical recitation by an actor'? And, as a last question, is it necessarily a virtue to stress the lyrical emotion which underlies a narrative poem rather than the external elements of the story?

To be fair, however, Dannreuther's comments should be considered in relation to their context. Subsequently, he makes some shrewd observations about Loewe's weaknesses. But quite apart from his half-hearted appreciation of the composer, it is easy to see that he connected the beginnings of the modern ballad as a musical art form with other essays in melodramatic music to illustrate recitation. The artistic problems confronting such music are discussed by him in the last two paragraphs of the same chapter. 'The unity of effect', he writes, 'was difficult, if not impossible to attain, because as the reciter's topic or his mood changes, the music must change—and as music must recur to its beginning or remain inchoate, the two aspects rarely fit together.' The fallacy in this statement is an important point in a later discussion.[1] For the moment, it will be enough to say that that is precisely the problem the modern ballad had to solve, and the elements of Loewe's method which I have summarized on page 49 offer a practical approach to it. It is not the only solution, as we shall see. However, there can be no doubt that the introduction of recitative as an artificial device avoids the problem altogether from one point of view, and completely ignores the lyrical fundamentals of the poetry. At the same time, *Die Lorelei* is not to be denied a place as a modern ballad because of the introduction of recitative. The device will be met again in the Russian ballads, when a different set of circumstances will arise. For all that, the likeness of *Die Lorelei* to a typical operatic scena carries its own implications.

Brahms's position in the development of the modern

[1] Chapter V.

ballad is by no means easy to define. It is very interesting to compare quotations from two distinguished Brahms scholars. Dr. Colles asserts[1] that 'the ballad style' (i.e. of the poetry) 'with its half articulate human feeling always stirred Brahms to peculiar sympathy. *Mädchenfluch* . . . is one of the most finely wrought of his ballads.' Turning to Fuller Maitland's essay on the composer,[2] a seemingly contrary opinion is expressed. 'In some few instances Brahms set to music narrative poems dealing with exciting events, but as compared with Schubert's or Loewe's productions in this class, *his are very few and unimportant.*' The italics are mine. Continuing, the writer goes on to say, '*Entführung* has the peculiarity, rare in his narrative songs, of being set to the same music for each stanza, not *durchcomponirt*; another, *Verrat*, is almost the only instance of a ballad dealing with active dramatic action, and it is a superbly successful one.' From their respective points of view, I think both critics are quite justified. Colles, of course, was dealing with the composer's reactions to certain styles of poetry. Fuller Maitland, on the other hand, was concerned only with the results of those reactions in relation to the modern ballad as a whole.

Brahms's setting of the Scottish ballad *Edward* was for two voices—as was also *Walpurgisnacht*—and linking these and the others of op. 75 with the Five Songs for one or two voices of op. 84 (including *Vergebliches Ständchen*) Colles writes:

'In all of them Brahms's idea is to use the voices semi-dramatically, carrying out the conversational structure of the ballads and making use of varied tone colour, alto and tenor in *Edward*, and alto and soprano in the several dialogues

[1] *Oxford History of Music*, vol. vii.
[2] Grove's *Dictionary of Music and Musicians*, vol. i.

between mother and daughter. In *Vergebliches Ständchen* there is not . . . any difference of tessitura for the two voices. That fact, together with the suggestion of naughtiness in the ballad, accounts for its superior attraction as a single-voiced song in recital programmes.'

The appropriateness of a duet setting for dialogue ballads is not to be denied, although there may be those who deem it an artificial device contrary to the original spirit of the poetry. That is a matter of little moment. *Vergebliches Ständchen* will maintain its fame as a solo ballad, and like the early *Liebestreu* offers ample proof of the composer's ability to present a dialogue narrative very effectively in solo form.

The important fact which arises from Brahms's treatment of the ballad is that he was never concerned with giving it any distinctive musical form as a ballad. Colles has remarked that 'Brahms generally accepted a poem not for any merit in itself, but because he felt a song to be lurking behind its rhythm, its fantasy, or its imagery'. Brahms's song forms were musically founded. They take into account the traditional differences between the *Volkslied*, the *volksthümliches Lied*, the strophic, and the *durchcomponirt* styles. Thus the excellent *Verrat* is *durchcomponirt*, *Entführung* is strophic; in *Murray's Ermordung* the form is simple ternary and the style strophic, and so on. Apart from the delightful *Vergebliches Ständchen*, his most characteristic ballad is, perhaps, *Das Lied vom Herrn von Falkenstein*. Here the thematic context is very definitely based on the dramatic characterization, and it falls quite conveniently into a ternary structure. A vigorous melody of eleven bars (C minor) serves for the opening three verses. In verse 4 this tune becomes the bass of the pianoforte accompaniment, while the vocal line is a counter-melody. A 'middle section', beginning in A flat and ending in E flat, serves for verses 5 and 6, and the remaining verses mark a return to the opening melody. 'As in a folk-song', writes Friedländer,[1] 'the same melody treats of supplication and suspense, of hope and fulfilment.' And the pianoforte part of this song is worth study, too. For all that, Brahms's nearest approach to the modern ballad style is in the comparatively little known *In der Gasse*, where the whole song is virtually derived from the first four bars.

Perhaps Friedländer has gone to the root of the matter when, in discussing *Treue Liebe*, he comments on 'the way in which the poem is changed from a ballad-like narrative to a finished, almost lyrically sustained song'. The ballad, as such, held no characteristic distinction for Brahms, although it often inspired him to write some expressive and very beautiful *lieder*. The histrionic changes of voice in *Vergebliches Ständchen*, *Liebestreu*, and *Von ewiger Liebe* call for vivid characterization on the part of the singer. These changes are not required in the duet ballads of op. 75, but these, in their different ways, are dramatically effective. It is significant, nevertheless, that the three solo ballads named are among the best loved of all Brahms's songs. The composer's use of the title for some of his instrumental works is discussed in a later chapter. But it is noteworthy that some of his song-groups, such as ops. 57, 59, 63, and 75, carry the vague title of 'Songs and Ballads', or 'Ballads and Romances', while op. 58, which includes *In der Gasse*, is entitled 'Songs and Romances', and op. 84, in which *Vergebliches Ständchen* appears, 'Romances and Songs'.

Before we leave the German ballad for its counterpart

[1] Max Friedländer, *Brahms's Lieder* (O.U.P.).

61

in other countries, there are at least three composers who must be considered, Hugo Wolf, Gustav Mahler, and Hans Pfitzner. Walter Ford has said of Wolf's ballads[1] that 'they are not the best Wolf. He seems to have relished them as a release from more serious work, and to have let his fancy run riot in a profusion of pictorial illustration in which no touch escapes his sharp and vigilant eye. Clever, effective, and brilliant they certainly are, but these are not words which rise to the lips in attempting to describe the best kind of music.' Later, the same writer confesses that he is 'plainly the wrong person to deal with Wolf in this department of his work, so will leave it to others'. This is a very frank admission, and quite in keeping with the forthright character of the writer. It is all the more modest because his essay is a splendid piece of criticism.

Actually, I think it is true that Wolf is at his best in the more intimate, the more personal lyrics; or in the monumental conception of a poem like *Prometheus*, for example. Indeed, from one point of view, certain ideals in his method of composition would seem to run counter to the spirit of the ballad as such. It is only necessary for me to touch very briefly on the fundamentals of Wolf's conception of song. It is original and individual enough to defy successful imitation, a fact which some modern song writers would do well to remember; and not infrequently it defeats analysis. His song forms are born of a remarkable fusion of the poetic and musical root-ideas; and often a song is cast in a form which is valid only for that particular poem.[2] For Wolf then, each ballad text

[1] *Heritage of Music*, vol. ii (O.U.P.).
[2] See Ernest Newman, *Hugo Wolf* (Methuen); and also the same writer's masterly notes for the Hugo Wolf Society.

would present its own problems of form and context and would be solved by him accordingly. Thus, while his methods might, and often did, give a ballad an astonishing individuality, they could not necessarily preserve that peculiar identity which belongs to ballad literature as a whole. This is neither a condemnation of Wolf's diversity of forms nor of the typical character of the ballad. We shall never find him attempting to fit the ballad into the form of a typical *lied*, nor into the artificial mould of an operatic scena. We may find him far transcending the comparatively simple methods of Loewe, and *evolving* from the detail of the narrative a definitive and unified dramatic scena. To those who would wish to preserve the ancient simplicity of the ballad in a modern art form, this may not seem to be as desirable as a less detailed and smaller scaled essay would be. Perhaps that was what Walter Ford felt when he left the discussion of Wolf's ballads for someone else.

To me, the situation is clearly expressed by saying that no one should go to Wolf for a typical ballad any more than they should for a typical *lied*. That you may find examples of both types among his songs is true enough, but only when, within the Wolfian scheme, certain poems happen to conform to such types. The songs of Wolf are not distinctive types; they are individual poems. That is, I think, the cardinal principle which underlies a true understanding of Wolf. In any event, the present position may be a little clearer if we take the opportunity of comparing settings of Goethe's *Der Sänger* by Loewe, Schubert, Schumann, and Wolf, not from any stupid motive of deciding which is best, because it is very doubtful if any one of the composers would have advanced this example as his best, or even as a representative song. Indeed,

it has been said that Wolf himself was far from satisfied
with his setting and hesitated about its inclusion among
the Goethe songs. But from a comparison of the four
songs, it will be interesting and helpful to discover the
angles of approach of each composer towards the ballad
as an art form.

*Der Sänger*, as Capell has said, 'is a ballad of idealised
medievalism'. It is by no means a satisfactory poem to
set to music. To quote Capell again, it is 'indeterminate,
because Goethe's poem leaves out the " thrilling strain"
with which the minstrel charmed the court and which
seems to be needed to form the core, not indeed of the
lyric, but of a musical composition on the subject'.[1]
Schubert's setting was the first of the Goethe songs which
he wrote in 1815. It is set in the conventional style
he inherited from his predecessors, Zumsteeg and Reichardt. There are frequent changes of tempo, and the vocal
line consists of alternations of recitativo and arioso
styles. For all that, it has some notable points of vivid
detail, and here and there, that lovable warmth of the
spontaneous Schubert. Loewe's ballad, composed in
1836, is conventional enough in style, but it has the merit
of cohesion, and within its limitations is an effective,
though somewhat undistinguished, setting of the poem.
A lively rustic melody in common time alternates with a
more undulating section in six-eight; then the latter is
elaborated in a somewhat artificial manner for the words
'Ich singe wie der Vogel singt . . .', and the opening melody
is recalled for a characteristic ending. The music at times
tends to be rather commonplace, but a good singer can
make it sound quite effective. Schumann's setting, composed in 1849, is in a rather shapeless *durchcomponirt*

[1] Capell, *Schubert's Songs* (Benn).

style, with a vocal line which is a curious amalgam of declamatory and lyrical styles. The pianoforte accompaniment is somewhat self-conscious and often rather obvious in its effect. Partly from its shapelessness and the lack of any unifying musical feature, and partly because of the odd mixture of styles, the ballad as a whole fails to escape a sense of monotony and unreality. Wolf wrote his setting in December 1888, and there is little doubt that the important pianoforte melody at the opening is the 'thrilling strain' which Capell has suggested should be the core of the musical setting. This effect is definitely realized when the voice takes over this particular melody at the words 'Ich singe wie der Vogel singt'. It forms, too, a characteristic unifying factor in the ballad as a whole. The vocal line, now dramatic, now lyrical, maintains a melodious declamation in which certain fragments of melody gain significant development as the song proceeds. The concluding twenty bars always seem to me to suggest a summing up of the thematic material, and it is not without its dramatic effect.

A sentence from Dannreuther's criticism of Loewe, quoted earlier, has a certain application here to both Schubert and Schumann. For the poetry definitely tells its own story, while the music is subordinate to the point of sacrificing the musical cohesion for the detail of the narrative itself. Loewe's musical form is very obvious, it is true, and the music is sometimes quite commonplace. But the formal definiteness has its advantages, and the 'musical actor' can lend it a certain degree of vividness. Loewe is more successful when his thematic material is directly founded on the dramatic features of a narrative. In this example the musical form has little connexion with the story, and a simple stanzaical ballad needs a more spontaneous melody than his. Wolf, with a far richer musical resource than Loewe, accomplishes the musical unity with a feature which is a fundamental of the poem. The vocal line is thus free to follow its expressive declamation, and the musical texture to develop its own formal identity.

In *Der Rattenfänger* Wolf gives us a descriptive pianoforte accompaniment which is both complete and continuous in itself.[1] Above it, the vocal line has a characteristic melodious freedom which, while it naturally falls into the stanzaical mould of the poem, never misses any of the subtleties of the story. The variations in the contrary-motion scale towards the end of each verse are worth noting; as are, too, the variations in the metrical rhythm. Each verse conveniently presents different aspects of the Rat-catcher's tale, and so Wolf was able to give a masterly and detailed expression to the colourful narrative within the broad outlines of a strophic ballad. Mörike's *Der Feuerreiter* is based on two main themes: '(a) that of the opening bars, which is developed symphonically as a symbol of the restless creature in whose blood the thought of fire acts as a poison; (b) the wild cry that always accompanies the words "Hinter'm Berg . . . in der Mühle"'.[2] Here is an example where Wolf has taken the apparent fundamentals of Loewe's method and with his own subtle dramatic instinct and uncanny sense of detail evolved an astonishing dramatic scena, the effect of which is enhanced in his own arrangement of the ballad for chorus and orchestra. Suggestions of folk-music are not very frequent in Wolf. They are generally to be found only when the poetic expression and feeling are intensified by

[1] Wolf orchestrated this in 1890.
[2] From Ernest Newman's notes for the Hugo Wolf Society, vol. vi.

such means. There may be a certain significance, therefore, in the fact that in so many of his ballads there are
traces of a sublimation of German popular melody.

The *Rheinlegendchen* of Gustav Mahler from *Des Knaben
Wunderhorn* is a delightful example of folk-song melody
vitalized and intensified by a nervous chromaticism and an
intriguing and vivid orchestral accompaniment. In many
ways, this is one of the most charming of Mahler's songs.
The simple strophic form and the colourful folk-song
style make an immediate appeal and render the narrative
in a natural and convincing manner. Pfitzner's ballad,
*Die Heinzelmännchen*, also has an admirably descriptive
orchestral accompaniment which 'imparts such remarkably
grotesque and intense life to the little dwarfs'.[1] It is a
ballad which deserves to be better known in England than
it is, for despite certain obvious traces of Wagnerian influence it has a distinct individuality of its own.

There is little point in carrying the story of the modern
German ballad any further.[2] Contemporary controversies
would only add new problems without solving any of the
old; moreover, some of the present-day German songs,
like those of Russia, have fallen under the sterile and
inartistic influence of current politics. In any case, there
is nothing in them which will add to or detract from the
main arguments of this essay. Happily, the German ballad
was not confined to its native frontiers.

It was Heine's *Es war ein alter König* which inspired
one of Grieg's best known ballads. A tiny strophic song,
it is derived from the opening unison and the succeeding
pianoforte bar. Its affecting simplicity is that of pure
folk-song. His setting of Björnson's *Die Prinzessin* is

---

[1] Weissmann, *The Problems of Modern Music* (Dent, 1925).
[2] Certain modern examples are considered in Chapter V.

equally successful. Again it is a strophic ballad, simple and sincere, and of the very essence of Scandinavian folk-song. It is very easy to see that Delius used it as an exact model for his *Twilight Fancies*. Another Scandinavian composer to be noted is the younger Stenhammer whose ballad *Florez and Blanchiflur* is a splendid song. Despite traces of German influence, the nationality of the ballad is never in doubt. And the simple folk-song idiom of the same composer's *Irmelin Rose* is just as effective. The Delius song, *Irmelin*, makes for an interesting comparison with that of the Swedish composer. Similarly, it is significant to compare Grieg's *Spielmannslied* with the Delius song, *The Minstrel*. Whether Ibsen's poem can be considered a true ballad is open to doubt. It is the minstrel's own story, it is true, but it is his emotional reaction to the event rather than the event itself which is the expressive feature of the poem. Both songs are in simple ternary form, with a quasi-recitative passage for the middle section. Paradoxically, fine song though it is, the Delius is somewhat reminiscent of a Stephen Adams ballad[1] on a higher artistic plane.

Because of the casual use of the term 'ballad' for all sorts of drawing-room songs in England it is necessary to remember my particular use of the title in considering examples of the modern English art ballad. I am restricting the term, as it should be restricted, to narrative songs of real artistic merit. There is no doubt that George Henschel's *Young Dietrich* can be considered to be one of the most effective examples of the modern art ballad in English. A powerful and vivid song, it is, as may be expected, in the style and manner of Loewe. So, too, are the same composer's lesser known examples, *Salome*, *The*

---

[1] Cf. *The Lute Player* (Allitsen), for example.

*Last Battle*, and *Der Schenk von Erbach*. There are two English women composers who must gain a very honourable mention here. Liza Lehmann's *L'Ankou* shows a dramatic sense of the highest order, and must be rated a very fine ballad indeed; while the *Ballad of the Bones* from Ethel Smyth's *The Wreckers* has a haunting melody which is quite distinctive.

The ever-popular *Salt-water Ballads* by Frederick Keel must not be forgotten. Of course, Masefield has undoubtedly used the term 'ballad' rather indiscriminately, but there is some significance in the fact that nearly all of the poems which he has collected under this title are descriptive rather than reflective, even when the real spirit of narrative is not there. Examples like Hurlstone's *Five Miniature Ballads* can hardly have their place here for the title is more or less nondescript, seeing that the songs are pure lyrics.

The names of Parry and Stanford must inevitably occur in discussing any phase of modern English song. Stanford's early song, *La Belle Dame sans Merci*, is a romantic ballad with an attractive Celtic flavour. On the other hand, his setting of Heine's *Die Wallfahrt nach Kevlaar* is a typical product of his German training, while scattered among his very many excellent songs one or two delightful Irish narratives may be discovered. It is this versatility of styles which is one of the most remarkable features of Stanford's music, although the Irish in him is never far away. · Nearly always in his instrumental works the influence of classical German models is very evident, while there is an undoubted suggestion of the eighteenth-century Italians in his Latin settings, such as the *Mass in G* and so on. His many effective choral ballads are mentioned elsewhere. Like his songs, they derive their lyrical charm and fluency very largely from his native folk-lore. His scholarly arrangements of Irish folk-song are well known and are, perhaps, a characteristic return for the inspiration he derived from them. The songs of Hubert Parry are decidedly lyrical in form and style, and his narrative songs present no unusual features. A scena for baritone and orchestra, *The Soldier's Tent*, must gain inclusion here, as well as such songs as *The Maid of Elsinore* and *The Laird of Cockpen*. There will be many to whom the last-named will seem the most characteristic example of the three.

Generally speaking, however, the tendency of English song is towards the purely lyrical, and impersonal narrative is rarely favoured by our better song writers. Narrative songs are to be found in abundance among English 'royalty ballads', a fact which is, perhaps, more significant than it seems. At the same time, there will be those to whom a poem like Housman's *Is my team ploughing?* will seem to have an affinity with dialogue ballads like *Liebestreu* and *Edward*, for example. This is a point of view which cannot be lightly dismissed and it must be considered more fully in a later chapter. As will be seen, it raises musical questions of some importance.

In French song the *ballade* is of far greater importance than the ballad; but the renaissance of the *ballade* in France is too wide a digression to be considered here. One of the most striking examples of a narrative song in French is Saint-Saens's *La Fiancée du Timbalier*, a lengthy ballad by Victor Hugo. It is set for mezzo-soprano voice and orchestra. Certain Wagnerian influences are not to be denied, but it is a highly characteristic work, and a most effective dramatic essay. The settings of Goethe's *King of Thule* by Berlioz and Gounod are to be preferred to the setting by Liszt, and each is typical of its composer.

And there are examples like the *Ballad of Queen Mab* from Gounod's *Romeo and Juliet* which must have their place here. Nearly always they are distinctly lyrical in style and present no unusual formal features.

The dramatic genius of the Russians remains to be considered, and a dozen or so examples of their ballads from Glinka (b. 1803) to Tcherepnin (A.) (b. 1899) should present a practical and comprehensive survey of the native peculiarities. For the Russian ballad indeed presents new features in style and treatment, although these may be, from another angle, only a more intensive application of old principles. Coming late into the stream of musical progress, Russian music held a certain novelty which it is not easy to define. Was it the strange mixture of Eastern and Western influences that the geographical position of the country gave to its music? Or was it the charm of a comparatively untutored and intensely national art? Was it that peculiar, and at times, theatrical vehemence in the musical expression? Or was it only the hypnotism of their sombre emotions, their sardonic humour, their bitter irony? All these were features which were bound to strike a new note in an art which had reached by devious routes the symphonic perfection of a Beethoven and the dramatic power of a Wagner.

But these are features which will have to be expressed in their musical terms, at least, so far as they are to be discovered in their ballads. The unique quality of their folk-song need not be analysed. It is evident, and it is easily recognized. But their attitude in the matter of musical declamation must be carefully considered. In Glinka's ballad, *The Midnight Review*, the rhythm of the vocal line is essentially declamatory—in this case, somewhat metrical—while the melodic elements are more clearly defined in the accompaniment. In effect, the vocal line is a series of short, recitative-like phrases, and the musical continuity is entirely preserved by the colourful accompaniment. But the important implications of this characteristic, which is frequent enough in Russian song, are more clearly revealed when the song is sung in the original language. Then it will be seen that the elements of the vocal line are to be found in the rhythms and inflexions of the language itself.

It was in pursuance of this same ideal that Dargomijsky, in his opera *The Stone Guest*, laid himself open to the gibe that it was 'a recitative in three acts'. But the power and vividness of his excellent ballads are not to be denied. There was always a certain Eastern intensity in all he wrote, and his technical mastery enabled him to go a step farther than his contemporary, Glinka, in his regard for the meaning and metre of the poetry. It was Cui who said of Dargomijsky's finest ballad, *Knight Errant*, 'it is impossible to put into adequate words all the laconic strength, the picturesque qualities, and the vivid realism conveyed by this song. It breathes the spirit of the past and appeals to the mind as vividly as a picture.' It is certainly a finely wrought ballad. The first three and last three bars suggest a very effective touch of dramatic unity. The *parlando* rhythm of the opening returns as a more clearly defined melody for the concluding verse, and the 'middle section' is a vivid expression of the swift action of the story. And the accompaniment throughout is a model of descriptive music.

On the other hand, the style of Borodin as revealed in his ballad *The Sleeping Beauty* is more definitely melodic, although it is just as colourful and effective. Here the thematic basis of the whole song is revealed in the opening vocal phrases and a descending whole-tone scale first heard in the pianoforte accompaniment towards the end of the second verse. It is this latter feature which goes to the making of an effective final cadence. In examples like *The Convoy* by Bleichmann, *When the King goes forth to war*, and *The King and the Jester*, both by Koenemann, we have the simple melodic charm of Russian folk-music with a colourful and descriptive accompaniment. Arensky, too, in his ballad *The Wolves*, maintains a fluent melodic line above a descriptive accompaniment, but his vocal line is more suggestive of the dramatic detail of the narrative than of the simple basis of folk-song, although his nationality is never far to seek.

But Modeste Moussorgsky was, perhaps, the greatest genius of them all. His was a very original mind, and in the matter of vocal declamation he was certainly influenced by his native speech rhythms and inflexions. Sometimes he was able to fulfil these ideals within the sturdy outlines of a quasi-folk-song melody, as in *Varlaam's Ballad* from his remarkable opera, *Boris Godounov*, where a colourful orchestral accompaniment only intensifies the vivid expression of the story. A similar fusion, in a lesser degree, is also seen in the satirical humour of his *Song of the Flea*, perhaps his most widely known song. The four dramatic songs known as *Songs and Dances of Death* have often been described as ballads, although each of the songs has a very distinctive character and style. The narratives, each and all, are thoroughly morbid and creepy, and Moussorgsky has succeeded in giving to the music a quality of grim realism. The first song, *Trepak*, is remarkable in many ways, not least because it seems to hold the very essentials of ballad music. The impress of folk-song and the spirit of the dance are there. The thematic origin of the whole song is undoubtedly revealed in the opening lento assai, an eerie recitative of a dozen bars or so. The declamatory fragments of the vocal line are destined to be developed into a typical folk-tune, while the tiny rhythmic figures in the pianoforte bass are ghostly hints of the national dance which Death invites the poor peasant to enjoy. The second song is entitled *Cradle Song*, but it is a strange lullaby. The scene is set in the tortuous chromatic quaver passage in octaves which serves as the pianoforte introduction, and the short declamatory phrases of the vocal line. At the lento funesto what may be termed the Death motif makes its first appearance. The stark dialogue then proceeds in free declamatory style, always suggesting, sometimes rather vaguely perhaps, the thematic background of the opening pianoforte bars and the distinctive Death motif. But the musical texture and its continuity are rather loosely held, and the song, as a whole, has the character of an effective essay in declamatory impressionism. It does not seem to possess that cohesion which is the inherent quality of pure narrative. In the *Serenade* the scene is again set in the introduction, a languorous chromatic vocal melody. Then comes the love-song of Death, in a familiar song form. It has a typical Russian flavour, and it is vivified by pungent chromaticisms. It ends with some declamatory phrases above a reiterated tonic pedal. *Field Marshal Death* is, in effect, a dramatic song in which the ejaculatory declamation of the battle scene finally yields to the quasi-folk-song of Death. Again the lack of cohesion is apparent, but given a vivid performance it is not so noticeable. Probably because some of the declamatory phrases of the earlier pages are vaguely re-echoed in the more definite melodic style of the concluding section.

Undoubtedly, it is the first of the four songs which is nearest to the ballad tradition. The second and fourth suggest the dramatic scena, while the third lives up to its title of a serenade. It must not be forgotten, however, that the poetic purpose of the songs is the presentation of Death in four distinct aspects. The important elements of the musical expression must therefore stress the character and the scene rather than the natural sequence of events. Thus, while the fundamental spirit of true narrative is evident enough in *Trepak*, in the other songs the event is enacted rather than related.

The elder Tcherepnin's setting of *Menaeceus* partakes of the elegy as much as the ballad. It is a singularly beautiful song. The poetic atmosphere is admirably realized, and the sentiment is never overdrawn. A highly expressive accompaniment and a simple, eloquent vocal line invest the fisherman's grief with a quiet dignity which remains in the memory long after the very beautiful final cadence. His son, Alexander Tcherepnin, shows the influence of Prokofiev in his pianoforte writing, and in *A Contented Man* the continuity of the musical texture relies mainly on a fluent and expressive accompaniment, while the vocal line, despite its suggestions of native melody, is essentially declamatory in origin. The song reflects the typical Russian delight in a sardonic form of humour. Napravnik, who emigrated from Prague to Russia at the age of 22, will probably be remembered more for his important and successful work for Russian opera than for his abilities as a composer. His music lacks individuality, because so many 'influences' went to its making. But his *Voyevode*, *The Cossack*, and *Tamara*, all for solo voice and orchestra, must be mentioned here, particularly the first of them.

The distinctive work of Czech composers in this phase of song is better approached through the many choral narratives which are discussed in the succeeding chapter. The *Twenty-Six Folk Ballads* of Janáček reveal a vivid, dramatic sense deeply influenced by an expressive nationalism. His musical idiom is terse and often somewhat ejaculatory, founded as it is on natural speech rhythms and inflexions. It is always highly individual in character and often it is really moving. Of these folk ballads, five are for male voice solo, chorus, and pianoforte and are to be linked with his important choral ballads which are considered later, six are for voice and pianoforte, and the remainder consist of *Robber Ballads* for voice and pianoforte, and *Folk Nocturnes* for two voices and pianoforte. All were written during the years 1906–16. The same composer's *Day Book of one who vanished*, a song cycle for tenor and contralto solo, female trio, and pianoforte, may seem to be more nearly related to such cyclic works as *Winterreise* and *Dichterliebe* than to the modern ballad. But the wider scope of the narrative, its dramatic presentation, and its logical continuity carry it away from the lyrical ideals of the Schubert and Schumann cycles, and in the words of Rosa Newmarch, 'it is a monodrama which shows a surer touch than Berlioz's *Lelio*; but it needs vivid interpretation'. Novák's *Child Ballad*, and *Mountain Ballad* for voice and pianoforte (or orchestra) and *The Soul of Jan Neruda* for bass voice and orchestra reveal a nationalism couched in modern terms with a subtle impressionism, and, by comparison with Janáček, a more lyrical style. Ostrčil shows the influence of Novák in *The Stranger Guest* and *A Child became an Orphan*, the first for tenor and the second for mezzo-soprano, and orchestra. Kunc's *There was a Duck by the Danube* for

76

alto voice and orchestra is not without suggestions of both Novák and Janáček.[1]

Finally, the Sibelius ballad, *The Ferryman's Brides*, for baritone or mezzo-soprano and orchestra, must be named here. It is a colourful and characteristic work and it may be significant that it dates from a period when the composer had already experimented with some improvisations for recitation, chorus, and orchestra. But although there may be traces in it of a 'popular northern balladry' the song is closely akin to his choral essays in the same genre which are discussed in the next chapter. There is little doubt that, in setting narrative or dramatic verse, Sibelius is more convincing when he has the larger resources of a choral texture at his command.

It should now be possible to indicate some of the more constant features which are to be discovered in the progress of the modern ballad. It is not very surprising that a typical folk-literature should nearly always betray the influence of folk-song. In the simple strophic ballads this feature is a marked characteristic; and it is hardly less definite in those ballads which tended towards the lyrical ideals of the *Romanze* and kindred forms. And its dramatic effectiveness is eloquently shown in the Russian and Czech examples. The evolution of a distinctive art form from Loewe to Wolf indicates the importance of a bold principal theme which can be repeated at appropriate points in the narrative, and the relative effectiveness of a secondary theme (or themes) to afford contrast and maintain continuity within the natural sequence of the story. At the same time, the lyrical element of the ballad could be, and often was, preserved without detriment to its dramatic presentation; and in this a vivid and descriptive

[1] See also *Five Moravian Ballads*, by Vyčpalek.

77

accompaniment was an important factor. Where the dramatic element tended to carry the setting into the domain of the operatic scena, the vocal line was often purely declamatory in origin and the musical cohesion, as well as the dramatic continuity, was relegated to the accompaniment. There, naturally, the wider resource and scope of the orchestra was a decided advantage. Incidentally, the varying methods of vocal declamation afford stylistic contrasts of real importance which are well worth studying independently. And they cannot be ignored in considering the broader essentials of musical form.

How far these several features suggest a distinctive form for the modern ballad as such will be the appropriate subject for argument in the fifth chapter of this book. There a few contemporary examples remain to be considered, and then the general conclusions which are to be drawn from the survey as a whole can be discussed at length.

## CHAPTER IV

# DIVERS BALLADS

IT has been truly remarked that 'choral music has the longest tradition of all established forms of the art'.[1] It is hardly necessary, however, to discuss here the wide diversity of choral forms, sacred and secular, accompanied and unaccompanied, which are manifest from the simple chorus to the elaborate organization of the cantata and oratorio. The choral ballad, in all its varying forms, is akin to the choral ode, and both may be regarded as typical products of musical romanticism. To seek for musical antecedents in an earlier epoch is not very helpful. Someone has said that the public choral society begins with Handel. In choice of material, that is, and not in actual date. For despite the existence of choral societies in the eighteenth century, the public choral concert was a characteristic delight of the nineteenth. And there, in England especially, the popular secular item was almost invariably a choral setting of a ballad or a similar poetic narrative.

But while the claims of the established choral festivals were a conspicuous influence in England, in Germany it was certainly the enthusiasm for Schiller and Goethe which developed the choral ballad. It was presented in divers forms and under varying conditions. A distinctive choral form for the ballad could hardly be established, if only for very practical reasons. The fundamental demands of a choral setting of any poem involve peculiar problems of texture and form. Apart from the obvious considerations of verbal accentuation and musical continuity, the

[1] *Oxford History of Music*, vol. vii.

formal elements of a choral as compared with a solo setting may so easily be elaborated and extended, if only by the interspersing of solo or soli paragraphs. And composers were not slow to take advantage of these opportunities.

To survey the choral ballad in anything like the detail of the preceding chapter is therefore not very practicable. In some cases it would mean going over much the same ground again; in others, it would require the consideration of certain choral forms and their development. Wolf's *Der Feuerreiter*, Schumann's *Vom Pagen und der Königstochter*, Brahms's *Rinaldo*, Liszt's *Die Glocken der Strassburger Münsters*, Stanford's *Revenge*, Parry's *Pied Piper of Hamelin*, Coleridge Taylor's *Hiawatha*, and, if you like, Walton's *Belshazzar's Feast*, are all choral narratives. But he would be bold who would find any other factor common to them all. And the list could be multiplied very considerably without any difficulty.

It is not a matter of answering the facetious question, When is a choral ballad not a cantata?—nor of discovering a supposed art form for the choral ballad itself. By its very nature the choral ballad was almost bound to develop, via the romance, into various forms of the dramatic cantata. The musical environment gave it every assistance. The trend of opera was towards the dramatic expressionism of the Wagnerian music-drama, the symphony and the concert overture towards the symphonic poem and programme music of various kinds. In such a swift-moving stream it followed the tide. Here and there a certain nationalism preserved a kind of identity, but structurally as well as expressively the dramatic element was a very significant feature.

An example like Wolf's *Der Feuerreiter* was frankly a

choral transcription of the solo setting. And there were other examples which fulfilled the formal and the stylistic features of the modern art ballad in a choral texture. But the wider scope offered by the cantata form could hardly be resisted, especially in the lengthy narratives. Its effectiveness is easily recognized, and its weakness is only apparent when the tendency to rely on a succession of choral and solo items ignored the strength of a cohesive whole. Moreover, it must not be forgotten that the choral ballad made its appearance at a time when the choral cantata had already established itself. Works like Beethoven's *Meeresstille*, Mendelssohn's *Walpurgisnacht*, Schumann's *Paradise and the Peri*, and Brahms's *Rinaldo* are milestones on a long road from Bach to, say, Blockx. Lastly, the leitmotive ideal of Wagner had its influence, and, obviously, it could be an effective means of maintaining the dramatic and musical continuity. At the same time, a composer like Stanford, while absorbing the musical influences of his training and his generation, produced a series of choral ballads in a characteristic style of his own.

It is a strange fact that although Schumann was able to make a comparative success of the lengthy *Paradise and the Peri*, in his several choral ballads—*Der Königssohn*, *Des Sängers Fluch*, *Das Glück von Edenhall*, all by Uhland; and *Vom Pagen und der Königstochter*, four ballads by Geibel—he failed every time. None has survived. His choral technique was always defective, particularly in extended choruses. The *Romances and Ballads*, ops. 67, 145, and 146, for unaccompanied chorus, were hardly more successful, and they show Schumann's tendency towards the style of the Romance rather than the dramatic ideals which were eventually to be such a significant feature in this phase of choral art. Brahms was much more

81

successful than Schumann in this form of composition, as *Schicksalslied*, *Nänie*, and *Gesang der Parzen* will show. Liszt's *Die Glocken des Strassburger Münsters* is a setting of the opening scene of Longfellow's *Golden Legend* for baritone solo, chorus, and orchestra, which follows, more or less, the style of Schumann. However, examples of the German choral ballad, frequently set for male voices, are plentiful enough. Perhaps those of Rheinberger—*Das Thal des Espingo*, *Wittekind* (both for male chorus and orchestra), *König Erich* (for mixed choir and pianoforte), and *Clarice Eberstein* (for soli, chorus, and orchestra)—may be named as typical examples of interesting mediocrity. On the other hand, Peter Cornelius's setting of Uhland's *Die Vätergruft* for baritone solo and mixed chorus may confidently be named as an outstanding example which Dannreuther has justly described as 'the most original piece of vocal programme music in existence'. And Reger's *Die Nonne* (for chorus and orchestra), Pfitzner's setting of Schiller's *Columbus* (for eight voices unaccompanied), Strauss's *Taillefer* (for chorus and orchestra), and Paul Graener's *Wiebke Pogwische* (for soli, chorus, and orchestra) may suffice as more modern examples, which are thoroughly characteristic of each composer.

Among the Russians the influence of nationalism and a tendency, in varying degrees, towards dramatic impressionism may be noted in such examples as Rimsky-Korsakov's *Ballad of the Doom of Oleg* (for soli, male voices, and orchestra), Kalinnikov's *Roussalka* (for soli, chorus, and orchestra), Rachmaninoff's setting of Poe's famous ballad *The Bells*, and Moussorgsky's *Destruction of Sennacherib* and *Joshua Navin* (all for chorus and orchestra).

Sibelius, many of whose earlier works were founded on *Kalevala*,[1] the epic of his country, e.g. the part-songs for male voices unaccompanied, has published but one choral ballad, *The Captive Queen*, for chorus and orchestra. But the superb work entitled *The Origin of Fire*, for baritone solo, male chorus, and orchestra, must surely earn a distinguished place here. It is interesting, too, that Mr. Cecil Gray's enthusiasm for the unpublished symphony, *Kullervo*, for soli, chorus, and orchestra, almost suggests that a ballad-like narrative could aspire, not only to the organization of a cantata, but the mighty proportions of a choral symphony.[2] One regrets that such a work is still in manuscript.

French choral ballads are not very numerous. One of the few works specifically entitled so is Berlioz's *Sara la Baigneuse*, which was originally written for male quartet and afterwards enlarged for chorus and orchestra. Often, however, choral settings of narrative and quasi-narrative poems are given such titles as eclogues, *poèmes lyriques*, *chansons*, and the like, and this, together with the varied qualities of the French choral cantata, typifies the somewhat characteristic attitude of the French towards choral music generally.

Two American composers must gain inclusion here. Chadwick's choral works with orchestra, *The Viking's Last Voyage*, *The Song of the Viking*, and *Lovely Rosabel*, are virile and imaginative choral ballads. Parker, whose oratorio, *Hora Novissima*, has won international recognition, shows no little power and skill in a series of choral ballads beginning with *The Ballad of a Knight and his*

[1] Which Longfellow so completely plagiarizes, even to the adoption of the peculiar metre, in his *Hiawatha*.
[2] Cecil Gray, *Sibelius* (O.U.P.).

*Daughter* and *King Trojan*, both dating from his student days in Munich. Thereafter there follow in steady succession *Normannenzug*, *The Kobolds*, *Harold Harfager*, and *King Gorm the Grim* for mixed chorus, *The Norseman's Raid* and *The Leap of Roushan Beg* for male chorus, with orchestral accompaniment in every case.

English choral ballads are plentiful enough. They range from the short, concise form in which Stanford was conspicuously successful to the dimensions of a secular cantata. Many called for soloists, and nearly all were set to an orchestral accompaniment. A great number were commissioned for the regular choral festivals which are such a feature in English musical life, and some have hardly survived their original performance. Not all have deserved the oblivion into which they have fallen. The vigorous *Sir Patrick Spens* by Pearsall is a splendid example from the first half of the nineteenth century when English choral music depended a good deal on glees and madrigals. Examples like Bridge's *Ballad of the Clampherdown* and *The Inchcape Rock* and Barnett's *Ancient Mariner* show little more than a pleasant mediocrity, but Erskine Allon's *Annie of Lochroyan* for soprano, chorus, and orchestra, to judge from contemporary opinion,[1] must have had no little beauty and originality. MacCunn and Mackenzie, both sons of the land of ballads, have contributed some interesting examples, the former with his *Lord Ullin's Daughter* and *Lay of the Last Minstrel*, while Mackenzie's *Dream of Jubal* includes a part for reciting voice. The same composer's *Cotter's Saturday Night* and his cantata, *The Story of Sayid*, must also be mentioned. Parry's *Pied Piper of Hamelin* is a

[1] Unfortunately, I have not been able to examine the score of this work.

distinguished and very effective example, and Walford Davies's *Hervé Riel* is never likely to lose its place in the choral repertoire. Coleridge Taylor's *Five Choral Ballads* of Longfellow have never won the universal recognition of his *Hiawa'ha*, but his *Tale of Old Japan* has had a certain popularity. Charles Wood's *Ballad of Dundee* is characteristic of a scholarly musician who always wrote effectively for chorus, while for humour Waddington's *John Gilpin* and Wallace's *Massacre of the Macphersons* (a burlesque ballad for male voices and orchestra) are thoroughly successful. The works of Stanford in this department are outstanding. *The Revenge, The Voyage of Maeldune, The Battle of the Baltic,* and *Phaudrig Crohoore* are all consistent in style and show a complete mastery of the concise form of the choral ballad. There is a real deftness in his handling of chorus and orchestra alike, his characteristic lyricism always charms, and his sense of dramatic effectiveness never falters. Havergal Brian's *Die Wallfahrt nach Kevlaar*, Grainger's *The Bride's Tragedy* and *Sir Eglamore*, Cyril Scott's *La Belle Dame sans merci*, Walthew's *Pied Piper*, Whittaker's *Lyke Wake Dirge*, and Holst's *King Estmere* may suffice as more recent examples. Choral ballads on the smaller scale of part songs for male and for mixed chorus are very numerous and no useful purpose would be served by enumerating random titles.

An impressive list of choral ballads by Czech composers deserves significant consideration. The choral traditions of Czechoslovakia—particularly of their male choirs—are of the highest quality. Indeed, it has been said that the true approach to the modern spirit in Czech music is through their choral works.[1] It was the nationalism of Smetana

[1] There is an interesting essay by Rosa Newmarch entitled 'Leos Janáček and Moravian Music Drama' in the *Slavonic Review* for December 1923.

and Dvořák which first placed this country—now, unhappily, the victim of Nazi domination—on the musical map. In some ways this nationalism has been intensified since then, as may be seen by comparing Smetana's choral ballad, *The Three Horsemen* (for male voices), Dvořák's *Hymnus* (for mixed voices and orchestra) and his cantata, *The Spectre's Bride* (for soli, chorus, and orchestra), with the later works enumerated below. The strange figure of a monk named Křižkowsky is the link. In his case, it was probably his monastic surroundings rather than the superiority of Czech male choirs which led him to write exclusively for men's voices. His ballads, *The Drowned Girl* and *The Recruit's Prayer*, together with a cantata, *Two Stars from the East*, are generally considered his finest works.

But more important than his actual compositions is the direct influence he exercised on Leos Janáček, undoubtedly the greatest Czech composer since Dvořák. His is a very individual genius, deeply rooted in nationalism, with a vivid, dramatic sense of expression, and a certain terseness in construction. His researches in the matter of 'speech-melody' are an important guide not only to his methods of vocal declamation but also to his melodic style generally. 'To every word the people utter', he says, 'is attached a fragment of the national life. Therefore the melody of their speech should be studied in every detail.' The ejaculatory style of his melody springs from this belief, and this, together with an unflinching realism and tense emotionalism, gives his music a powerful and compelling expressiveness. The three choral ballads to the words of Peter Bezruc, the Silesian labour poet, are set for male voices, unaccompanied. They are *Marycka Magdonova* (written in 1908), *Seventy Thousand* (1911), and *Teacher Halfar* (1917). They have been described as 'miniature music dramas, not intended to be enacted on the stage, but in the imagination'. In the present servitude of the Czechs these ballads will have an added reality. Three more of his choral ballads must be named. *At the Inn of Solan* calls for a solo voice, male choir, and orchestra. It was written in 1912. *The Czech Legions* (written 1919) is set for unaccompanied male chorus, while the *Ballad of Kaspar Rucky* (1922) is for women's voices.

In the choral ballads of Novák—*The Accursed Daughter*, *The Murderer Lover*, and *The Unhappy War* (all for chorus and orchestra)—there is not the tense verism of Janáček. Instead he tends towards impressionism and his style is more polyphonic. Ostrčil is represented by *The Legend of St. Zita* for tenor solo, chorus, orchestra, and organ; and *A Czech Christmas Legend* for male chorus unaccompanied. And Kunc has a setting of *Seventy Thousand* for chorus and orchestra. Few will deny that these are all significant contributions to the development of the choral ballad. The provision of an English text for some of them is certainly to be hoped for, although in the case of Janáček there would be difficulties to be overcome.

Before passing on to the consideration of instrumental ballads, mention must be made of certain forms of melodramatic music (i.e. music written to accompany a reciting voice) in so far as they have been inspired by ballad poetry. This form of composition has never really established itself, although its popularity in some countries, notably Bohemia, must be recognized. The criticism of Dannreuther quoted on page 58 is indicative of the mildly scornful attitude of some sections of musical opinion towards it. The pioneer efforts of Rousseau and Benda, however, have the classical authority of Beethoven in his *Egmont* and *Fidelio*.

Schumann's *Schön Hedwig* and *Vom Haideknabe*, both by Hebbel, as well as his *Die Fluchtlinge* (from Shelley), are set for pianoforte. So, too, are the six examples by Liszt, of which the best known are *Lenore* (Bürger) *Der Traurige Mönch* (Jokai), and *Der Blinde Sänger* (Lenau). Strauss's setting of *Enoch Arden*, a singularly interesting piece of work, is also for pianoforte, while Schilling's *Jung Olaf* is set for pianoforte or orchestra. Among English examples are Corder's *The Minstrel's Curse* for orchestra, and Stanley Hawley's *The Bells* and *The Raven*, both for pianoforte. Mackenzie's use of a reciting voice in *The Dream of Jubal* has already been mentioned. The device has been used in several modern works of various kinds, e.g. Walton's *Façade*, Bliss's *Morning Heroes*, Honegger's *King David*, and Milhaud's *Christophe Colombe*.

The popularity of melodrama in Bohemia ever since the days of Benda has produced a wide variety of works of this kind. Perhaps the most ambitious is Fibich's trilogy *Hippodameia*, for orchestra. The same composer's *Hakon* must also be included here. Foerster's many examples are all very interesting. *Norwegian Ballad* and *The Three Riders* are typical. Ostrčil's *Ballad of the Dead Cobbler* and *A Czech Ballad* are also fine examples, set for orchestra.

Instrumental ballads present a bewildering variety. Those for orchestra are obviously to be classified as programme music. It will be seen that they may be entitled orchestral ballads, tone poems, symphonic poems, symphonic ballads, and so on. Dukas's *L'Apprenti Sorcier* is an orchestral scherzo based on Goethe's poem, and

Strauss's *Till Eulenspiegel* is certainly narrative music. Examples like Mackenzie's *La Belle Dame sans Merci*, MacCunn's *Ship of the Fiend*, Somervell's *Helen of Kirkconnell*, Drysdale's *The Spirit of the Glen*, Parker's *Northern Ballad*, Chadwick's *Tam O'Shanter*, Von Bülow's *Des Sängers Fluch*, and Petersen-Berger's *Florez and Blanchiflur* are specifically entitled orchestral ballads. And the list could be extended easily enough. On the other hand, Janáček's *Ballad of Blanik* and Ostrčil's *Tale of Semik* are called symphonic poems, while Tchaikovsky's *Voyevode* is a symphonic ballad. And Somervell's *Thomas the Rhymer* is an orchestral suite. But there is no need to make this an orchestral catalogue. These are examples of programme music which carry the implications of their poetic basis in their titles. It is only when the bare title of ballad is used that the position is not so explicit. For there must be noted that tendency to apply 'the title to any piece of no very defined form but having a certain romantic feeling'. That is a vagueness which gives the word no significance at all. It is not a matter of great moment, perhaps, but for the purpose of this essay it is not possible to discover how far these instrumental ballads are inspired by ballad poetry when the title is so loosely used.

The first of Brahms's four ballads, op. 10, was certainly based on the Scottish ballad *Edward*, and the Intermezzo op. 117 was inspired by *Lady Anne Bothwell's Lament*. Chopin's ballads are generally supposed to have been based on the poems of Mickiewicz. Novák's ballad *Manfred*, for pianoforte, declares the source of its inspiration in the title, and there may be a certain significance in the fact that Grieg's Ballad is a series of variations. But in very many cases the title carries no especial significance, and suggests no distinctive musical form. The fact that Chopin's ballads are all in compound duple time is interesting but, from our point of view, not very informative. It is only necessary to choose at random such contrasted examples as Dvořák's ballad for violin and pianoforte, Henschel's for violin and orchestra, Leo Sowerby's for two pianos and orchestra, Vieuxtemps's Ballad and Polonaise, and Křenek's Tango-Ballad to realize how difficult it would be to establish any stylistic feature which is common to all instrumental ballads. In short, this manifestation of the ballad is best regarded as poetic or programme music of a more or less indefinite form, and unless the poetic basis is explicitly disclosed, the title must be considered as nondescript.

It would be an easy matter to conclude this chapter with a scornful denunciation of the 'drawing-room' (or 'royalty') ballad. But the primary purpose of this essay is to consider where and why the title of ballad is used in music. And with regard to this species of popular song we can forget for the moment the slur implied by the adjectives 'drawing-room' and 'royalty'. The former is innocuous and the latter quite reprehensible. As we have seen, the title of ballad has often been applied in poetry to designate the popular, irrespective of whether it was narrative or not. It is possible that this may explain its usage in the present case. At the same time, the prevalence of rhymed narrative among these songs is not to be discounted. I have said 'rhymed narrative' because in so many cases the words amount to very little more than mere versification. Often the work of a professional lyric-writer, rather than a poet in the accepted sense of that term, these lyrics were quite deliberately constructed so as to provide the composer with every opportunity for easy and tuneful setting. On the face of it, this may seem harmless enough. Such popular songs must always have a place in a country's music. But when these products are raised to an undeserved status and importance it calls for very vigorous protest. We have only to reflect that less than eighty years ago Sullivan was·appointed professor of pianoforte and *ballad singing* at the Crystal Palace School of Art to realize the extraordinary position attained by this form of song. It was regarded, in fact, as characteristic English song.

Braham's *Death of Nelson* was written about ten years after the birth of another Nelson, the composer of *Rose of Allandale*, *The Pilot*, and very many more ditties of the same kind. The drawing-room ballad had begun its long reign. It mattered little that at least half a dozen gifted song writers appeared within the next twenty or thirty years. They were all engulfed by this craze for popular songs. Hatton, who could write such splendid songs as *To Anthea* and *The Enchantress*, and a real ballad like *Simon the Cellarer*, found the Nelson touch more lucrative. Loder, whose song *The Brooklet* rivals Schubert's setting of the same poem, could sink to the depths of *The Diver*, mainly because of an impossible contract to produce one song a week for his publisher. Pierson's songs, like the composer, never won the affections of his countrymen, although his abilities were certainly recognized abroad. Bennett, following the Mendelssohnian cult, kept himself more or less aloof from the shop-ballad, although his songs are somewhat shallow. Bache, with more real ideals than many of his contemporaries, might have stopped the rot had he lived longer. But the promenade concerts of Julien were the fashion, and the reforms of August Manns had only just begun. And so to Sullivan with his *Lost Chord*, *The Absent-minded Beggar*, and similar banalities which are in such contrast to his *Orpheus with his lute* and the other Shakespearian songs. Clay's *I'll sing thee songs of Araby* and *The Sands of Dee* are another tiny break in the murky horizon. But the renaissance of English song had to wait for Stanford and Parry, although it was one of their contemporaries, Frederick Cowen, who was responsible for *The Better Land* among dozens of similar songs. Meanwhile the pile was always increasing with the productions of good, bad, and inferior musicians. Things like *The Volunteer Organist*, *Ora pro nobis*, and those of a more pretentious style like *The Holy City*, *Thora*, *Nirvana*, *The Trumpeter*, and so on were creating that enormous stock of so-called ballads on which the reputations of so many of our most eminent singers principally rested. It is a dismal record, for which composers, publishers, singers, and public must share the blame.

It has been said that the drawing-room ballad 'implies a composition of the slightest degree of musical value nearly always set to three verses (neither more nor less) of conventional doggerel'. There are exceptions, but only to the number of verses. It is not so much a form as a phase of English song and its former importance is steadily passing away. The modern counterpart of these songs can often lay claim to an improved musical craftsmanship, and no one will deny them their proper place in vocal literature. But one regrets that the title of ballad is still applied to such songs, for it loses all real significance. Even when the lyric is a narrative of sorts it exercises no influence on the ideals of the song in any way. And for precisely the same reasons that one has deplored the use of the title 'ballad' to describe any kind of popular poetry, so its use to designate popular vocal music is to be criticized. For the renaissance of English song may well develop a distinctive type of narrative song as characteristic as the German *Balladen*, and then we shall regret the debased currency of a title which should be as honourable as it is old.

## CHAPTER V

## CONCLUSIONS

TO reduce the varied musical activities so far surveyed to the limits of a concise and cogent summary would seem to be almost an impossible task. It is true there would be little difficulty in classifying the multiplicity of forms in which the ballad in music has been manifest, but any such categories as could be devised would be purely arbitrary. Moreover, they would have to be broad enough to admit the widely contrasted examples of contemporary composers in this phase of music. For example, Van Dieren's early work, *Belshazzar*, and Howard Ferguson's two ballads, *A Lyke Wake Dirge* and *The Twa Corbies*, are all set for baritone and orchestra, but that is the only feature common to both composers. Their styles are fundamentally different. The one is a peculiarly original composer, the other offers a modern valuation of familiar characteristics. From Germany, too, comes such contrasted works as Kurt Weill's *Ballade vom angenehmen Leben*, Křenek's *Ballade vom König Lobesam*, and Schreker's *Die Glühende Krone* from the opera *Der Ferne Klang*. Despite certain similarities in the formal aspects, these three examples are vastly different in style and effect. The wilful absorption of current features of popular music, a forbidding pseudo-contrapuntal style, and a harsh delight in harmonic dissonance are rather obvious dissimilarities which must be analysed on their own terms. And, to name only one more solo ballad, there is the characteristic *Lud Gidea* by the Bulgarian composer, Vladigeroff, which offers an effective amalgam of native folk-song, Wagnerian music-drama, Russian pungency, and an extension of Loewe's *balladen* style. Among choral ballads it may be enough to cite the wide gulf between such works as Benjamin Britten's *Ballad of Heroes* and Armstrong Gibbs's *Ballad of Gil Morrice*. Obviously, then, the individuality of the ballad in music is not to be discovered in a general classification of various musical forms which are, in any case, the current products of widely different artistic epochs.

Even if such a summary were considered feasible it would give to the purely musical features a precedence which is denied by the order of the nouns in the title of this book. Indeed, if the method were carried to a logical conclusion the characteristic factor of the ballad text would have very little significance at all. A symphonic poem is a symphonic poem whether its inspiration be a ballad or an epic. Similarly, the formal lineaments of a choral ode or cantata remain very much the same whether the verbal text is a ballad or not. And despite the nonsense which has so often been written about song-forms, these may be classified logically enough, with a typical ballad in almost every category!

Alternatively, of course, it would be possible to enumerate certain formal and stylistic features which are to be discovered, in greater or lesser degree, in a large number of musical ballads and to suggest, on the basis of these, a characteristic art-form for the ballad in general. Such an artificial postulate could be founded only on very fallacious reasoning, and in attempting to prove too much it would prove nothing at all. Some of the finest ballads would have to remain as exceptions to a rule which has no foundation in fact.

The more logical approach to the subject will be, of course, through the ballad itself. Earle Welby's remark (already quoted) that 'ballad does not differ from ballad as a poem by Shelley differs from one by Keats' is a sufficient reason for such a procedure. The poetic postulate can be accepted as it stands. There is no need to ask why certain poetic values of the ballad are constant. But if the ballad in poetry possesses a marked identity, why should the translation of this poetic individuality into music produce a diversity of forms? That, surely, is the fundamental inquiry, and out of it will probably come a proper understanding of the expressive subtleties (and not the mere structural design) of musical forms.

At once it will be recognized that the instrumental ballad, by its very nature, cannot be approached through the poetry. It does not translate the detail of the poetic context; it expresses only its general effect. The ballad is the subject of inspiration; it is not the ruling factor. As a phase of musical romanticism, some of the examples of programme music which are founded on ballads may show some interesting similarities—in the predominance of folk-song melody, for example, or in certain features of musical impressionism—but the ultimate analysis of all such manifestations of the ballad in music must be founded on musical considerations only. The situation may be made clearer by a simple analogy. A prose version of a poem must inevitably be analysed as prose and not according to the characteristic poetic values of the original.

Examples of the ballad in melodrama are more directly controlled by the verbal context for the very simple reason that the music must accompany the actual recitation of the poetry. Even so, the musical context itself is still free to develop its intrinsic form within the dramatic scope of the story, although it need not be unduly hampered by the poetic detail. Dannreuther's doubts in this matter have already been quoted (page 58), but they proceed from a false premiss. It will be observed that he assumes a prescribed form for the music ('as music must recur to its beginning or remain inchoate'), so that, unless this form coincides with the natural sequence of the narrative, 'the two aspects rarely fit together'. It is not clear whether he is stressing the ternary ideal in form or the necessity for a return of the original tonality in order to conclude a musical movement. It is certain, however, that the principles of musical form are far subtler.

So as not to anticipate later arguments, the fallacy of his statement may be demonstrated by an example taken, not from a ballad, but from a simple lyric by Mörike, *Ein Stündlein wohl vor Tag.*

> Derweil ich schlafend lag
> Ein Stündlein wohl vor Tag
> Sang vor dem Fenster auf dem Baum
> Ein Schwälblein mir, ich hört' es kaum
> Ein Stündlein wohl vor Tag:
>
> Hör' an, was ich dir sag',
> Dein Schätzlein ich verklag':
> Derweil ich dieses Singen tu',
> Herzt er ein Lieb in guter Ruh',
> Ein Stündlein wohl vor Tag.
>
> O weh! nicht weiter sag'!
> O still! nichts hören mag!
> Flieg' ab, flieg' ab von meinem Baum!
> Ach, Lieb und Treu ist wie ein Traum,
> Ein Stündlein wohl vor Tag.

Both Franz and Wolf offer settings of this poem which strictly preserve the strophic form, but their expression of the poetic emotion is fundamentally different. The Franz song, from the point of tonality, is in simple ternary form. As the second stanza consists of the message given by 'the swallow who sang outside the window just before daybreak', the musical form is entirely justified. Wolf, however, realizing that each verse conveys a growing intensity, and that the last verse is far removed emotionally from the first, just because of the swallow's message, has evolved a far more significant form. He does so by a subtle use of tonality. Each verse modulates a semitone higher and the song ends out of the key. No singer can escape the expressive consequence of this subtlety; no listener can fail to realize the poetic truth which has engendered the musical form. No one will say the music is inchoate because it ends on the dominant chord. You can prove the utter rightness of Wolf by adding the tonic chord (with or without the *tierce de picardie*); it completely spoils the song, and entirely destroys the balance and significance of the musical form.

There are other details, of course, which ought to be noted in analysing these songs, but I have deliberately concentrated on the actual outline. The formal principles simply expressed here are capable of considerable extension and complexity. It is important, therefore, that they should be fully appreciated, and the reader should do the comparative analysis himself with the actual music.

To return to the problems of music melodrama, it is clear that the limitations suggested by Dannreuther need have no existence. The music can be given a thoroughly logical form and still express the progress of the drama. In effect, therefore, it will probably be a kind of symphonic poem accompanying the recitation, the declamatory rhythm of which must be provided for in some way or another. It is this latter factor, more than any, which must be counted as the real drawback against success in melodrama. The recited lines and their rhythmic connexion with the music can be indicated only very loosely. Lacking not only the melodic contour but also the exactness of a vocal line, it is almost impossible to escape a peculiar detachment between the spoken declamation and its musical accompaniment. At the same time, the success of the Czech composers in this phase of music is especially noteworthy; and the close relation of these essays with certain characteristic aspects of Czech opera is highly significant.

Now the ballad would seem to possess just those very features which make for successful melodrama. It maintains, generally, a swift sequence of events and a terse action; it expresses powerful elemental passions with, very often, a simple human interest; and in the simplicities of its poetic lineaments are all the essential qualities for effective declamation. Here and there, national or local patriotism or the warm fervency of a political faith only adds to the force of the poetry. But if the ballad makes for expressive melodrama, it is also true to say that in its intrinsic poetic features are qualities which tend to lead, inevitably, in another direction. As the ancient minstrel often found in the lilt of a well-loved tune the simple metre of his rhymed improvisation, so the modern actor may often find that the repetitive rhythm and rhyme of a ballad will carry his reciting perilously near the realm of simple song. For if the vitality of a language is rhythmic, its expressiveness is fundamentally melodic.

This calls to mind the forceful ideals of Janáček in this direction. It is significant that he comes of a country where music-melodrama is more definitely practised than anywhere else in the world. Janáček's verism in speech-tone may hold a deeper interest and influence for a future generation than it does for us. For present purposes, however, it may be accepted as an intensification of methods which were already characteristic of the Russian composers, and, more particularly, of Moussorgsky. Not that the Russian was as concerned as Janáček was with the stark expressionism and the inherent individuality of speech-melody. The Czech sought to transmute verbal eloquence into melody, while Moussorgsky aimed at the reverse process, transmuting melody into verbal eloquence. The result, in certain circumstances, is not very dissimilar, as a comparison of *Kat'a Kabanova* and *Boris Godounov* would tend to reveal. But in other works, the opera *Jenufa*, for example, Janáček's use of a 'characteristic figural kind of tone-speech . . . fractional motives', as it were, from which sometimes the longer melodies could be evolved, is not to be identified with the ejaculatory declamation of Moussorgsky. Both are highly individual attempts to solve the intrinsic problem of song-writing, and each must be set against the background of its own circumstances. Incidentally, it is only necessary to study Moussorgsky's song-cycle *Sans Soleil* to see the manner in which his declamatory methods profoundly influenced the smoother lyricism of Debussy and Ravel.

In the Russian ballad two schools of thought are clearly manifest; and they may be discerned almost side by side in the respective works of the Tcherepnins, *père et fils*. The disciples of Glinka, heavily indebted to nationalist influences, are generally lyrical in style and ideal in character. In the dramatic style and realistic character of Dargomijsky and Moussorgsky, the folk-song influence is not so direct. With the former it often serves as the bare melodic outline into which the rhythmic subtleties of his vocal declamation are effectively fitted, while the musical continuity follows very vividly the dramatic trend of the narrative. Moussorgsky's vocal line, on the other hand, is often more ejaculatory in effect and fragmentary in style, as it fulfils the declamatory inflexions of the verbal text. Generally, his unerring dramatic sense succeeds in maintaining an effective musical continuity although by the slenderest thread, as, for example, in *Field Marshal Death*. In other examples, like *Varlaam's Ballad*, his method is similar to that of Dargomijsky. Two factors which are always lurking in the shadows behind all the Russians must be noted—their preoccupation with sociological and political ideals, and their delight in histrionic effect. They give a characteristic timbre to their ballads as they do to their songs.

The circumstances surrounding the German *Balladen* were very different. Here it was not the vocal expression of a group of composers building their music anew on nationalist foundations. Instead, it was a distinct phase in what is, perhaps, the greatest song literature in the world; and the *Lied* itself was born of a mature musical impulse. It is important to recognize, too, the peculiar features of German ballad poetry, particularly because it partook of both the classicism and the later romanticism which were characteristic of German literature during the century beginning about 1740. Broadly speaking, therefore, it was not folk-poetry in the sense that so many of our old ballads were, but, rather, the re-creation of much the same ideals by poets who were themselves subject to distinctive cross currents during a significant epoch in their country's literature—a great age, for it included both Schiller and Goethe. Fortunate in this natural inheritance, the German ballad in music was no less so in its subsequent career.

When the late Dr. Cummings writes:[1] 'Besides the many ballads among Schubert's songs, those of Zumsteeg and Carl Loewe may be referred to as having helped to fix the type of German ballad that reached its ultimate perfection in Brahms', it is clear that conciseness has been gained at the expense of cogency. The German ballad can neither be explained nor dismissed in a single sentence. It is a phase of song which runs through the whole history of the modern *Lied* and it was subject to the same changing influences.

Conveniently enough, *Balladen* fall into three well-defined groups—the strophic, the romantic, and the dramatic. That the first-named should exhibit very strongly the impress of the *Volkslied* is significant but not surprising. It might be considered, in fact, as a re-creation of the old minstrel ballad by a reverse process. It is, in short, a simple ballad, so simple that it needs either the spontaneous melody of a Schubert or the charm of a folk-song to make it really eloquent. To many this form will seem to express the true ballad ideal and undoubtedly it does come nearest to the ancient form. But it must be remembered that while the inspiration of German ballad poetry was ancient enough it was expressed in a variety of forms, some of which were essentially contemporary in style and character. In certain aspects, it manifests a reaction against classicism and a distinct tendency towards romanticism. This rather implies that the romantic ballad was the fitting medium for its musical expression. In many cases this is undoubtedly true. But the romantic ballad, which reached its highest expression in Schumann and, more particularly, in Brahms, often suggests a curious duality of aims. For the vocal line is rendered with all

[1] Grove, *Dictionary of Music and Musicians*, vol. v.

the graceful elegance of the *Romanze*, while the dramatic features of the narrative are subtly expressed in a vivid accompaniment. There is every justification for the method, for while the vocal line fulfils the fundamental lyricism of the poetry, the effect of the narrative is intensified by the musical context. And it could all be encompassed within a shapely and well-defined musical form. The dramatic ballad, on the other hand, aims at a more graphic, declamatory vocal line, and seeks its form in the dramatic needs of the story rather than in purely arbitrary musical essentials.

While it is a convenient generalization to say that the dramatic features of the romantic ballad are concentrated in the pianoforte accompaniment, the vocal line is not to be dismissed as being wholly undramatic in effect. The differences between Schumann and Brahms in this respect are noteworthy. It will be observed that when Schumann attempts the melodramatic he rarely succeeds. Perhaps the crisis and conclusion of *Belshazzar* may be cited as his most graphic attempt in vocal declamation. More often, his quasi-recitative effects tend to disturb the natural flow and symmetry of the music without adding very materially to its dramatic significance. Brahms, on the other hand, while preserving the melodic essentials of his vocal line, often succeeds in being more expressively dramatic. But the long sweeping phrases which are so characteristic of his *lieder* often give place, in his ballads, to a vocal melody which is made up of short and sequential fragments, as in *Liebestreu*, for example, with a consequent gain in intensity and expression.

The dramatic ballad, in its earlier stages, reveals an attempt to render the narrative with all the vividness of dramatic vocal declamation while at the same time fulfilling some of the formal lineaments of the *lied*. Zumsteeg, with his alternations of recitative and arioso passages, was obviously aiming at a dramatic vocal utterance, but only at the expense of the formal unity of the music. Even Schubert, as the disciple of Zumsteeg, was hardly any more successful, although his natural genius asserts itself in some singularly effective passages. But the youth of eighteen, allowing the divine spontaneity of his music to discover its own intrinsic form, gave us the astonishing *Erlkönig*. Happily for us, Schubert did not need a ballad text to reveal the profundities of dramatic vocal writing.

Loewe's *Edward* marks the turning-point in the progress of the dramatic ballad. Helped by the clear outline of a dialogue narrative, the thematic development is musically and dramatically logical. Here, as in Brahms's *Liebestreu*, the two characters are contrasted thematically, but the subsequent development in each case affords a striking example of the differences in style and method between the romantic and dramatic ballad. Loewe's consistency in his treatment of the ballad must not be taken to mean that all his ballads are dramatic. Some are purely strophic, and in these the impress of folk-song is very distinct. None are romantic, mainly because, vocally, they are all declamatory in utterance and dramatic in expression. The declamatory nature of his vocal line is undoubtedly derived from his experience as a singer, and his imaginative power reveals a rare poetic insight. His methods and ideals were destined to be expressed with a profounder subtlety by Wolf. And the very fact that Loewe's ballads can so worthily be compared with the work of the last of the great Meistersinger is indicative of their high artistic achievement. Between Loewe and Wolf there came that far-reaching influence on all forms of poetic music which is epitomized in the work of Richard Wagner. The excesses and eccentricities of certain contemporary examples add nothing to the progress of the German ballad beyond a distinct harshness and confusion of styles.

Two phases of influence are to be seen in the modern English ballad.[1] Many are heavily indebted to the romantic ballad. Even Henschel, who was nearest in spirit to Loewe, could not escape the influence of Brahms. Others, impressed with a folk-song idiom, exhibit a characteristic form of song which is often thoroughly successful. But the dramatic ballad, as such, is not favoured by English composers. Our song writers rarely forgo the melodic concept of a vocal line, and few have the courage to attempt the expressive declamation which is the outstanding feature of some of Hubert Foss's *Seven Poems by Thomas Hardy*, for example. How far this composer could apply the same dramatic technique to a solo setting of a ballad text remains to be seen. His *Castlepatrick* is a ballad-like song, strophically expressed, in colourful folk-song terms. It will be appropriate to mention here the vivid setting of Housman's *Is my team ploughing?* by C. W. Orr. In place of the usual stanzaical setting followed by other composers in this poem, Orr has approached the eerie dialogue in much the same way as Loewe in *Edward*. The thematic identity of the two 'speakers' is first established, and the musical development thereafter fulfils the growing dramatic intensity perfectly. For my own part, I shall always regard this song as an unexpected but thoroughly effective dramatic ballad. The poet meant it to be so.

[1] The drawing-room ballad is obviously excluded from consideration here.

To sum up, it may be remarked that this threefold classification of the solo ballad holds a more positive logic than may be apparent. It is clear that the strophic ballad fulfils the historical factor in a very definite way: by re-creating, in the reverse process, the actual creative process of the ancient minstrel. Its claim to be regarded as a typical ballad form is therefore very strong. In the romantic ballad the predominance of the musical factor is unmistakable. Here the narrative is expressed within a convenient musical form while the dramatic features of the story are concentrated in the accompaniment. The poetic factor is the ruling force in the dramatic ballad, and the definitiveness of a modern art form for the ballad is the result. The ballad in music has need of all three. Each and all, in their several ways, have produced masterpieces. Finally, the national factor must be reckoned with always. Ballad poetry will always be racy of the soil which begat it. Its musical translation cannot escape that influence which, as in the Russian and Czech ballads, for example, sometimes invests the music with a very remarkable individuality.

It is obvious that all these observations on the solo ballad will govern their actual performance. Unfortunately, far too many singers continue to regard any song simply as a means for the exhibition of vocal ability rather than the expression of an artistic unity and ideal. Thence arise the gross exaggerations which are committed in the name of 'interpretation', but are more accurately described as pure sensation. Real histrionic ability with the vocal means to sustain it are required for the adequate performance of the dramatic ballad. To apply the same melodramatic expression to a romantic ballad would be quite out of place. Here declamatory vividness must give place to melodic intensity and the lyrical fundamentals of both poetry and music duly preserved. The apparent simplicity of the strophic ballad is deceiving. It is almost like telling the story without gesture or costume to help the illusion. But the conditions are precisely those of the ancient minstrel who built his art on a simple affection for a well-loved tune and the direct appeal of his poetry. It is not unlikely that even a modern audience, for all its sophistication, will be strangely moved by the same simple sincerity of expression.

Earlier it was suggested that the choral ballad may be considered as an extension (in choral terms, of course) of the same fundamental principles which have already been discussed in connexion with solo ballads. This generalization is probably more positive than it may seem. The actual dimensions of the score must not be allowed to mislead one. A part-song setting of a narrative poem may reveal all the organization of a dramatic ballad, while the lengthier form of a cantata may simply express the lyrical formula of a strophic ballad. Moreover, it is important to remember that some of the innovations and developments in choral forms during the past century have a purely musical significance quite independent of the actual verbal text. For example, the succession of separate solo and choral movements which characterizes a familiar form of choral cantata has tended to give place to the closer coherence of a more unified form. There are important details with regard to verbal accentuation to be noted also. The indiscriminate and illogical repetition or omission of words is less frequent in the modern choral texture. These and other refinements in the technique of choral writing, together with the varying influences of instrumental forms and the Wagnerian music-drama, have a far-reaching effect on the progress and development of choral music generally, quite apart from the nature and style of the literary text which is used. Once these features are regarded in their true perspective it will be recognized that the choral ballad falls into much the same classification as that of the solo ballad. The strophic ideal is obvious enough in the simpler forms of choral ballad from the familiar part-song to the lyrical cantata. And there are many ballad texts which are perfectly suited to this treatment and no other. The romantic tendency is probably seen at its best in the closely knit organization of the form so splendidly achieved by Stanford and others. The influence of instrumental forms gives a conciseness and unity to the choral texture, while a well-wrought orchestral accompaniment lends a vivid expression to the dramatic event. Dramatically, the choral setting of a narrative poem may be as effectively rendered within the dimensions of a normal part-song as it is in the extended form of a dramatic cantata like *Hiawatha*. There will be those who profess to see little difference between the romantic and dramatic choral ballad. Others will suggest (sometimes a little too easily) that the influence of Wagnerian leitmotive is the distinguishing characteristic of the latter. But there are obvious reasons why the distinctions between the romantic and dramatic styles, in their choral forms, can never be so pronounced as they are in solo forms. It may be possible to imagine a choral declamation which is as graphic as that of a single vocal line—some of Janáček's choral ballads, for example, come very near to it—but there are obvious limitations. Expressively, the intensity of a choral form into which a dramatic story is moulded may not differ very materially from the vividness of a choral form which is definitely evolved from the dramatic sequence itself. There will be fundamental differences, nevertheless, however subtle though they may be.

Fortunately, the main object of this book has not been to assess or to decide musical controversies but rather to review the character and importance of the ballad in music generally. The extent and the variety of this phase of music would seem to be self-evident; its influence and its successes have been shown to be hardly less apparent. Its distinctiveness has been somewhat undermined by the abuse of the title. That it should be used to describe romantic forms in instrumental music with only a vague poetic basis is bad enough. But it is almost sheer infamy that so ancient and honourable a title should continue to designate popular songs of all kinds. The ballad has a character, a form, and a power which are rarely, and then only quite accidentally, suggested in such ditties.

The future of the ballad in music is not so clear. Admittedly, the story-teller's art is never likely to lose its popular appeal, but whether the simple lineaments of ballad poetry can survive in the complex organization (or disorganization) of the modern world is another matter. Naturally, its translation in musical terms is subject to the same doubts. However, there is no reason for one to indulge in rash prophecy. This book must stand or fall by the claim that, to adapt Earle Welby's words, the ballad in music is worthy to be studied, not as a really or reputedly very ancient curiosity nor as a peculiar musical product, but as a vital and permanently interesting form of poetic music. If that object has been achieved, then the considerable catalogue of music which has been discussed in these pages may be safely left to discover and determine its own future.

# BIBLIOGRAPHY

THIS list of books for further study is divided into the two categories of 'Critical Studies' and 'Collections'; and each is further subdivided under the headings of 'Poetry' and 'Music'.

## I. CRITICAL STUDIES

### A. *Poetry*

W. P. KER: *On the History of Ballads* (vol. iv of Proc. of Brit. Acad.).

F. B. GUMMERE: *The Popular Ballad.* 1907.

T. F. HENDERSON: *Scottish Vernacular Literature.* 1908.

—— *The Ballad in Literature.* 1910.

These are authoritative and important essays on the subject.

FRANK SIDGWICK: *The Ballad.* 1914.

An essay in the 'Art and Craft of Letters' Series.

SIR A. QUILLER-COUCH: *Studies in Literature: First Series.* 1918.

Contains a 25-page essay with quotations, criticism, and a study of the rival theories of origin.

LOUISE POUND: *Poetic Origins and the Ballad.* 1921.

ROBERT GRAVES: *The English Ballad.* 1927.

The latter contains a 30-page critical survey and some 34 examples including soldier-songs of the War.

W. J. ENTWISTLE: *European Balladry.* 1939.

See also the introductions to Scott's *Minstrelsy*, and to the *Roxburghe Ballads*: and chap. xvii, vol. ii, of *Cambridge History of English Literature*.

### B. *Music*

*Oxford History of Music.* Introd. vol., and vols. ii, vi, and vii.

E. WALKER: *A History of Music in England.* 1924.

H. WYLDE: *Music in its Art-mysteries.* 1867.

An essay by a former Gresham Professor of Music with chapters on the minstrels and their music.

ED. DUNCAN: *The Story of Minstrelsy.* 1904.

One of the 'Music Story' Series. An interesting if somewhat lengthy essay, containing a useful bibliography.

# BIBLIOGRAPHY

PIERRE AUBRY: *Trouvères et Troubadours.* 1910.

J. J. JUSSERAND: *English Wayfaring Life in the Middle Ages.* 1925.

> See also Essay on Ancient Minstrelsy in Chappell's collection of National English Airs (1838), &c.

A. B. BACH: *The Art Ballad; Loewe and Schubert.* 1890.

FULLER-MAITLAND: *English Music in the XIXth Century.* 1902.

A. HERVEY: *French Music in the XIXth Century.* 1902.

ERNEST NEWMAN: *Hugo Wolf.* 1904.

HUBERT PARRY: *The Art of Music.* 1920.

RICHARD CAPELL: *Schubert's Songs.* 1928.

M. FRIEDLANDER: *Brahms Lieder.* 1928.

*The Heritage of Music* (ed. Hubert J. Foss). 2 vols.

GERALD ABRAHAM: *Studies in Russian Music.* 1936.

CALVOCORESSI and ABRAHAM: *Masters of Russian Music.* 1936.

J. W. HENDREN: *A Study of Ballad Rhythm.* 1937.

E. M. GAGEY: *Ballad Opera.* 1937.

See also articles in Grove's *Dictionary of Music and Musicians* (ed. Colles, 1940) and *Oxford Companion to Music* (Scholes, 1939) under 'Song', 'Ballad', 'Ballad Opera', &c.

## II. COLLECTIONS

Only British and American ballads are noted here. For other European countries see under each country in *Titles of Collections of Ballads* in vol. v of Child's collection noted below and also in the bibliography on pages 229–38 of the introductory volume of the *Oxford History of Music.*

### A. *Poetry*

*Minstrelsy of the Scottish Border* (WALTER SCOTT). 1802–3.

> An edition (1902) edited by Henderson extends to 4 vols.

*English and Scottish Popular Ballads* (F. J. CHILD). 5 vols. 1882–98.

> The greatest and most important collection of ballads ever prepared.

*Roxburghe Ballads* (CHAPPELL and EBSWORTH). 1868–99. Vols. i–ix in 10 books.

> A collection of 16th- and 17th-century ballads with a wealth of information in the introductions to the several volumes.

# BIBLIOGRAPHY

*English and Scottish Ballads* (SARGENT and KITTRIDGE). 1904.

Some 300 ballads taken from Child's great collection with notes, criticism, glossary, and bibliography.

*Oxford Book of Ballads*. 1910; rev. 1932.

The best collection for the general reader.

*Reliques of Ancient English Poetry* (PERCY). 1765.

There is an edition in 2 vols. in Everyman's Library.

*Ballads* (FRANK SIDGWICK).

Fifty ballads with notes and a 30-page survey.

*Ballads and Ballad Plays* (HAMPDEN). 1931.

*Ballads Ancient and Modern* (MACINTYRE). 1929.

Two small but excellent collections.

*A Bundle of Ballads* (HENRY MORLEY). 1891.

A small collection with an interesting introduction.


B. *Music*

*Musical Century: One Hundred English Ballads* (HENRY CAREY). 1737.

*Legendary Ballads* (ed. BISHOP). 1828.

*National English Airs* (CHAPPELL). 1838.

*Old English Ditties* (CHAPPELL). 2 vols. 1881.

*Old English Popular Music* (CHAPPELL). 2 vols. 1893.

These three collections are excellent and contain informative introductions.

*English Songs of 17th and 18th Centuries* (HULLAH). 1871.

*Traditional Ballad Airs* (W. CHRISTIE). 2 vols. 1876, 1881.

*Songs and Ballads of the West* (BARING-GOULD and SHEPPARD). 4 vols. 1889–91.

*Traditional Tunes* (KIDSON). 1891.

*Songs of the Four Nations* (SOMERVELL). 1892.

*Manx Ballads and Music* (MOOR). 1896.

*Manx National Songs* (GILL and CLAGUE). 1896.

*Songs and Ballads of North England* (REAY and STOKOE). 1899.

*Ancient Irish Music* (PETRIE and STANFORD). 2 vols. 1902.

*The Minstrelsy of England* (DUNCAN). 1905.

*English Songs of the Georgian Period* (KIDSON and MOFFAT). 1907.

*Welsh Melodies* (LLOYD WILLIAMS and SOMERVELL). 1907.

## BIBLIOGRAPHY

*Songs of the Hebrides* (KENNEDY FRASER). 3 vols. 1909–21.

*North Country Songs, Ballads, and Pipe Tunes* (WHITTAKER). 2 vols. 1921.

*Ballads of Britain* (JOHN GOSS). 1937.

*American Ballads and Folk Songs* (LOMAX). 1934.

*American-English Folksongs from the Appalachian Mountains* (SHARP). 1917.

*Bayou Ballads* (MONROE).

*Ballads, Love-Songs, and Tragic Legends* (NILES). 2 vols.

*Songs of the Hill-Folk* (NILES). 2 vols.

*Beech Mountain Folk-Songs and Ballads* (MATTESON and HENRY).

# GRAMOPHONE RECORDINGS AND
# GENERAL INDEX

*With a Note by* MAURICE BROWN

In the following index you will find listed every composition that the author has cited in the text of his book. I have added to those which have been recorded for the gramophone an artist's name and a record number; a labour which I gladly undertook with all the enthusiasm of a proud godparent.

Once upon a time Dr. Northcote stood up in a public place and uttered some very plain words about 'obnoxious ballads'. Because of this I asked him to give a series of broadcast talks illustrated with gramophone records about the objects of his scorn. He did, and very quickly proved there was a vast literature of ballads which were anything but obnoxious. The unworthy examples were suitably treated.

This book was the natural consequence of those successful talks. It was therefore largely my fault that he came to write it, and it is obviously my duty to carry this baby.

It is never an easy task to find gramophone records to illustrate the music mentioned in a scholarly essay of this kind. Inevitably, the author writes of works which the recording companies have not thought it worth their while to perpetuate, or of music of which they have never heard. To be less hard on these enterprising institutions it should be added that they must exist to make money, and rarities do not sell.

Thus it has come about that I have had to take what I can and be thankful.

Many of these recorded ballads are not all that they should be. We find that the only recording of a certain Grieg song is sung in Italian; that piano is often replaced by orchestra, and orchestra by piano; that women sing men's songs and vice versa. At their best, such recordings can give but a poor idea of the original.

But some ballad composers, notably Loewe, are well represented in the lists, and the singers are excellent. For these we rejoice.

I have not hesitated to put down records which are difficult to obtain. Some are from Society issues, many are from foreign catalogues. A few no longer exist in any catalogue, but can perhaps be found in those shops which sell second-hand records if the purchaser has sufficient diligence and patience to make the search.

There are many gaps in the lists. Records of choral and orchestral ballads are few, and ballad opera is represented only by *The Beggar's Opera*. Once there were recordings of extracts from *Hugh The Drover*, but I doubt whether they can be found to-day. Pleasures such as Ramsay's *The Gentle Shepherd*, Arne's *Love in a Village*, and the operas of Shield, Hook, and others remain a remote dream to record collectors.

I hope that one day these voids may be filled by some courageous gramophone company. Meanwhile, we can only wait and see. M. B.

## CHAPTER II.  EARLY BALLADS

| | | |
|---|---|---|
| *Arthur O'Bradley* | | |
| *A-hunting we will go* | Boys' Choir | H.M.V. B 8201 |
| *Barbara Allen* | O'Doherty | REGAL-ZONO. |
| | | MR 248 |
| *Brave Lord Willoughby* | | |
| *Chevy Chase* | | |
| *Greensleeves* | | |
| *Heartsease* | | |
| *Roger de Coverley* | | |
| *The First Day of Xmas* | | |
| *Vicar of Bray* | Robertson | H.M.V. B 3971 |
| *Who killed Cock Robin?* | American Version, Mackinlay | COLUMBIA DB 651 |
| *Widdecombe Fair* | Robertson | H.M.V. B 3668 |
| *Willow willow* | | |
| *Young Henry Martin* | Tanner | COLUMBIA FB 1569 |

The following recordings of sea shanties will be of interest:

| | |
|---|---|
| Royal Naval Singers | COLUMBIA DX 699 |

    *Billy Boy; Johnny come down to Hilo; I'll go no
    more a-roving; Rio Grande*

John Goss                         H.M.V. B 2646
   *Shenandoah*
John Goss                         H.M.V. B 2831
   *Sally Brown; Hanging Johnny; Whiskey Johnny;*
     *The sailor likes his bottle-o; Clear the track,*
     *let the bullgine run*

ARNE
  *Come away, Death*
  *Despairing beside a clear*
   *stream*
  *Miller of Mansfield*

BRAHAM
  *Death of Nelson*       Widdop         H.M.V. D 1833

DAVY
  *Bay of Biscay*         Robertson      ,,    B 8081

DIBDIN
  *Ben Backstay*
  *I sailed from the Downs on*
   *the Nancy*
  *Jolly Young Waterman*    Titterton     DECCA K 617
  *The Lamplighter*
  *Tom Bowling*          Titterton     DECCA K 615

HGOK
  *The lass of Richmond Hill*   Smith       DECCA F 2067

LEVERIDGE
  *Roast beef of old England*
  *All in the Downs*
  *Black-eyed Susan*

PERCY
  *Wapping old stairs*

SHIELD
  *Death of Tom Moody*
  *The Wolf*           Allin        COLUMBIA DX 450

THE BEGGAR'S OPERA
  *Marquesita, Nelis, Ranalow,*
   *Walker, Heather, etc.*        H.M.V. D 524–6
  *Audrey Mildmay, Michael Redgrave,*
   *Roy Henderson, etc.*         H.M.V. C 3159–66

## CHAPTER III. MODERN BALLADS

ARENSKY
  *The Wolves*

BERLIOZ
  *King of Thule*        Berthon      H.M.V. C 2404

BLEICHMAN
  *The Convoy*

BORODIN
  *The Sleeping Beauty*

# GENERAL INDEX

**BRAHMS**
  *Das Lied vom Herrn von Falkenstein*
  *Edward*
  *Entführung*
  *In der Gasse*
  *Liebestreu* — Schnabel — H.M.V. DA 1294
  *Mädchenfluch*
  *Murrays Ermordung*
  *Treue Liebe* — Ginster — H.M.V. DB 1926
  *Vergebliches Ständchen* — Kipnis — „ DB 2998
  *Verrath* — „ — „ DB 2999
  *Von ewiger Liebe* — Onegin — „ DB 1485
  *Walpurgisnacht*

**DARGOMIJSKY**
  *Knight Errant*

**DELIUS**
  *Irmelin* — Evans — DECCA F 5707
  *Twilight Fancies* — Perli — COLUMBIA L 2344
  *The Minstrel*

**GLINKA**
  *Midnight Review* — Chaliapin — H.M.V. DB 933

**GOUNOD**
  *Ballad of Queen Mab* — Endrèze — PARLOPHONE
    *(Romeo and Juliet)* — E 11129
  *King of Thule* — Rethberg — H.M.V. DB 1456

**GRIEG**
  *Es war ein alter König*
  *Die Prinzessin* — Talamo (in Italian) — COLUMBIA DQ 850
  *Spielmannslied*

**HENSCHEL**
  *Der Schenk von Erbach*
  *The Last Battle*
  *Salome*
  *Young Dietrich*

**HURLSTONE**
  *Five Miniature Ballads*

**JANÁČEK**
  *Twenty-six Folk Ballads*
  *Day Book of one who vanished* (Song Cycle)

**JENSEN**
  *Edward*

**KEEL**
  *Salt-water Ballads* — Falkner — H.M.V. B 2917

**KLENAU**
  *Ebbe Skammelsen*

**KOENEMAN**
*The King and the Jester*
*When the King goes forth* Chaliapin      H.M.V. DB 1068
  *to War*

**KUNC**
*There was a Duck by the*
  *Danube*

**LEHMANN**
*L'Ankou*

**LISZT**
*Der Alpenjäger*
*Die Drei Zigeuner*      Scheidl      POLYDOR 27203
*Der Fischerknabe*
*Die Lorelei*      Onegin      H.M.V. DB 1291
*Die Vätergruft*
*Es war ein König in Thule*      Brunskill (in English)      COLUMBIA 9687

**LOEWE**
*Archibald Douglas*      Scheidl      POLYDOR 95215
*Der Sänger*
*Der Wirthin Tochterlein*      Katman      ODEON 2603
*Edward* ⎫
        ⎬    Bender      H.M.V. EH 827
*Erlkönig* ⎭
*Heinrich der Vogler*      Scheidl      POLYDOR 95213
*Herr Olaf*      Bender      H.M.V. EH 904

**MAHLER**
*Rheinlegendchen*      Schlusnus      DECCA CA 8082

**MOUSSORGSKY**
*Songs and Dances of Death*      Rosing      PARLOPHONE SW 4
                             ,,       ,,    SW 5
*Song of the Flea*      Chaliapin      H.M.V. DB 932
*Varlaam's Ballad*      ,,      ,,    DA 891

**NAPRAVNIK**
*The Cossack*
*The Voyevode*
*Tamara*

**NOVÁK**
*Child Ballad*
*Mountain Ballad*

**OSTRČIL**
*A Child became an Orphan*
*The Stranger Guest*

**PARRY**
*The Laird of Cockpen*      Robertson      H.M.V. B 3477
                                       (withdrawn)

*The Maid of Elsinore*
*The Soldier's Tent*

PFITZNER
  *Die Heinzelmännchen*
SAINT-SAËNS
  *La Fiancée du Timbalier*
SCHUBERT
  *Der Fischer*
  *Der Gott und die Bajadere*
  *Der Sänger*
  *Der Schatzgräber*
  *Der Taucher*
  *Der Tod und das Mädchen*    Allin (in English)    COLUMBIA 5019
  *Der Zwerg*                  Mysz-Gmeiner          POLYDOR 21454
  *Die Burgschaft*
  *Einsamkeit* (Mayrhofer)     Hüsch                 H.M.V. DA 1345
  *Erlkönig*                   Schlusnus             POLYDOR 67051
  *Hagars Klage*
  *Johanna Sebus*
  *Ritter Toggenburg*
SCHUMANN
  *Belshazzar*
  *Die Beiden Grenadiere*      Janssen               H.M.V. DB 3024
  *Die Löwenbraut*
SIBELIUS
  *The Ferryman's Brides*
SMYTH
  *Ballad of the Bones* (*The
    Wreckers*)
STANFORD
  *La Belle Dame sans Merci*
  *Die Wallfahrt nach Kevlaar*
STENHAMMER
  *Florez and Blanchiflur*
  *Irmelin Rose*
TCHAIKOWSKY
  *Edward*
TCHEREPNIN (A.)
  *A Contented Man*
TCHEREPNIN (N.)
  *Menaeceus*
VYCPALEK
  *Five Moravian Ballads*
WAGNER
  *Der Tannenbaum*
  *Die Beiden Grenadiere*
  *Senta's Ballad*             Rethberg              H.M.V. DA 1115
WOLF
  *Der Feuerreiter*            Rehkemper             DECCA LY 6022

| *Der Rattenfänger* | Rehkemper | DECCA PO 5063 |
| *Der Sänger* | | |

## CHAPTER IV. DIVERS BALLADS

### Choral

| | |
|---|---|
| BARNETT | *Ancient Mariner* |
| BEETHOVEN | *Meeresstille* |
| BERLIOZ | *Sara la Baigneuse* |
| BRAHMS | *Gesang der Parzen* |
| | *Nänie* |
| | *Rinaldo* |
| | *Schicksalslied* |
| BRIDGE, J. F. | *Ballad of the Clampherdown* |
| | *Inchcape Rock* |
| CHADWICK | *Lovely Rosabel* |
| | *The Song of the Viking* |
| | *The Viking's Last Voyage* |
| COLERIDGE TAYLOR | *Five Choral Ballads* (Longfellow) |
| | *Tale of Old Japan* |
| | *Hiawatha* Royal Choral Society { H.M.V. C 1931–4 |
| | (Cond. Sargent) { „ C 2210–3 |
| CORNELIUS | *Die Vätergruft* |
| DVOŘÁK | *Hymnus* |
| | *The Spectre's Bride* |
| ERSKINE ALLON | *Annie of Lochroyan* |
| GRAENER | *Wiebke Pogwische* |
| GRAINGER | *Sir Eglamore* |
| | *The Bride's Tragedy* |
| HAVERGAL BRIAN | *Die Wallfahrt nach Kevlaar* |
| HOLST | *King Estmere* |
| JANÁČEK | *At the Inn of Solan* |
| | *Ballad of Kaspar Rucky* |
| | *Marycka Magdonova* |
| | *Seventy Thousand* |
| | *Teacher Halfar* |
| | *The Czech Legions* |
| KALINNIKOV | *Roussalka* |
| KŘIZKOWSKY | *The Drowned Girl* |
| | *The Recruit's Prayer* |
| | *Two Stars from the East* |
| KUNC | *Seventy Thousand* |
| MACCUNN | *Lord Ullin's Daughter* |
| | *Lay of the Last Minstrel* |
| MACKENZIE | *Dream of Jubal* |
| | *The Cotter's Saturday Night* |
| | *The Story of Sayid* |

# GENERAL INDEX

| | |
|---|---|
| MENDELSSOHN | *Walpurgisnacht* |
| MOUSSORGSKY | *Destruction of Sennacherib* |
| | *Joshua Navin* |
| NOVÁK | *The Accursed Daughter* |
| | *The Murderer Lover* |
| | *The Unhappy War* |
| OSTRČIL | *Czech Christmas Legend* |
| | *Legend of St. Zita* |
| PARKER | *Ballad of a Knight and his Daughter* |
| | *Harold Harfager* |
| | *King Gorm the Grim* |
| | *King Trojan* |
| | *Normannenzug* |
| | *The Kobolds* |
| | *The Leap of Roushan Beg* |
| | *The Norseman's Raid* |
| PARRY | *Pied Piper of Hamelin* |
| PEARSALL | *Sir Patrick Spens* |
| PFITZNER | *Columbus* |
| RACHMANINOFF | *The Bells* |
| REGER | *Die Nonne* |
| RHEINBERGER | *Clarice Eberstein* |
| | *Das Thal des Espingo* |
| | *König Erich* |
| | *Wittekind* |
| RIMSKY-KORSAKOV | *Ballad of the Doom of Oleg* |
| SCHUMANN | *Das Glück von Edenhall* |
| | *Der Königssohn* |
| | *Des Sängers Fluch* |
| | *Paradise and the Peri* |
| | *Romances and Ballads*, ops. 67, 145, 146 |
| | *Vom Pagen und der Königstochter* |
| SCOTT | *La Belle Dame sans merci* |
| SIBELIUS | *The Captive Queen* |
| | *Origin of Fire* |
| | *Kullervo* |
| SMETANA | *The Three Horsemen* |
| STANFORD | *Battle of the Baltic* |
| | *Phaudrig Crohoore* |
| | *The Revenge* |
| | *Voyage of Maeldune* |
| STRAUSS | *Taillefer* |
| WADDINGTON | *John Gilpin* |
| WALFORD DAVIES | *Hervé Riel* |
| WALLACE | *Massacre of the Macphersons* |
| WALTHEW | *Pied Piper of Hamelin* |

| WALTON | *Belshazzar's Feast* | H.M.V. C 3330–4 |
| WHITTAKER | *Lyke Wake Dirge* | |

## Orchestral

CHADWICK
  *Tam O'Shanter*
DRYSDALE
  *Spirit of the Glen*
DUKAS
  *L'Apprenti Sorcier*  Toscanini  H.M.V. D 1689
JANÁČEK
  *Ballad of Blanik*
MACCUNN
  *The Ship of the Fiend*
MACKENZIE
  *La Belle Dame sans merci*
OSTRČIL
  *Tale of Semik*
PARKER
  *Northern Ballad*
PETERSEN-BERGER
  *Floręz and Blanchiflur*
SOMERVELL
  *Helen of Kirkconnell*
  *Thomas the Rhymer*
STRAUSS
  *Till Eulenspiegel*  Boult  H.M.V. DB 2187/8
TCHAIKOVSKY
  *Voyevode*
VON BÜLOW
  *Des Sängers Fluch*

## Instrumental

BRAHMS
  *Ballades*  Backhaus  H.M.V. DB 1897
  *Intermezzo*, op. 117  „  „  DB 2805
CHOPIN
  *Ballades*  Cortot  H.M.V. DB 2024/6
DVOŘÁK
  *Ballad for violin and piano-
    forte*
FAURÉ
  *Ballade*  Tagliaferro  H.M.V. W 984/5
GRIEG
  *Ballade*  Godowsky  COLUMBIA LX 9/10
HENSCHEL
  *Ballade for violin and
    orchestra*

122

KRENEK
   *Tango-Ballade*

LISZT
   *Ballade B minor*            Kentner          COLUMBIA DX 851/2

NOVÁK
   *Manfred. Ballad for piano-*
      *forte*

SOWERBY
   *Ballad for 2 pianos and*
      *orchestra*

VIEUXTEMPS
   *Ballad and Polonaise*       Swaap           H.M.V. C 4865

## *Melodramas*

BEETHOVEN
   *Egmont. 'Schluss-Monolog'*  Ebert          ODEON 11641
   *Fidelio*

BLISS
   *Morning Heroes. 'Spring*  Maine         DECCA F 5219
     *Offensive'*

CORDER
   *The Minstrel's Curse*

FIBICH
   *Hippodameia*
   *Hakon*

FOERSTER
   *Norwegian Ballad*
   *The Three Riders*

HAWLEY, STANLEY
   *The Bells*
   *The Raven*

HONEGGER
   *King David*

LISZT
   *Der Traurige Mönch*
   *Der Blinde Sänger*
   *Leonore*

MILHAUD
   *Christophe Colombe*

OSTRČIL
   *Ballad of the Dead Cobbler*
     *and the Dancing Girl*

SCHILLING
   *Jung Olaf*

SCHUMANN
   *Die Flüchtlinge*
   *Schön Hedwig*
   *Vom Haideknaben*

# GRAMOPHONE RECORDINGS

STRAUSS
  *Enoch Arden*
WALTON
  *Façade*                  Lambert, Sitwell       DECCA T 124/5

## *Drawing-Room Ballad*

| | | |
|---|---|---|
| *Absent-minded Beggar* | | |
| *Holy City* | Crooks | H.M.V. DB 1798 |
| *I'll sing thee Songs of Araby* | Oldham | „ B 4321 |
| *Nirvana* | Crooks | H.M.V. B 3630 |
| *Ora pro nobis* | Herwin | COLUMBIA DB 1951 |
| *Rose of Allandale* | Brunskill | COLUMBIA DD 388 |
| *Sands of Dee* | | |
| *Simon the Cellarer* | Allin | COLUMBIA 9807 |
| *The Better Land* | Ackland | H.M.V. C 2060 |
| *The Diver* | Allin | COLUMBIA DX 270 |
| *The Enchantress* | Brunskill | „ 9088 |
| *The Lost Chord* | Crooks | H.M.V. DB 2571 |
| *The Lute Player* | Dawson | H.M.V. C 2698 |
| *The Pilot* | | |
| *The Trumpeter* | Williams | COLUMBIA 9045 |
| *Thora* | Kullman | „ DB 1439 |
| *To Anthea* | Santley | „ 360 |
| *Volunteer Organist* | Dawson | H.M.V. B 3630 |

## CHAPTER V. CONCLUSIONS

| | |
|---|---|
| ARMSTRONG GIBBS | *Ballad of Gil Morrice* |
| BRITTEN | *Ballad of Heroes* |
| FERGUSON | *Lyke Wake Dirge* |
| | *Twa Corbies* |
| FOSS | *Seven Poems by Thomas Hardy* |
| | *Castlepatrick* |
| KŘENEK | *Ballade vom König Lobesam* |
| ORR | *Is my team ploughing?* |
| SCHREKER | *Die Glühende Krone* |
| VAN DIEREN | *Belshazzar* |
| VLADIGEROFF | *Lud Gidea* |
| WEILL | *Ballade vom angenehmen Leben* |

PRINTED IN GREAT BRITAIN BY
JARROLD AND SONS, LTD., EMPIRE PRESS, NORWICH